Asian American History: A Very Short Introduction

VERY SHORT INTRODUCTIONS are for anyone wanting a stimulating and accessible way into a new subject. They are written by experts, and have been translated into more than 40 different languages.

The series began in 1995, and now covers a wide variety of topics in every discipline. The VSI library now contains over 450 volumes—a Very Short Introduction to everything from Indian philosophy to psychology and American history and relativity—and continues to grow in every subject area.

Very Short Introductions available now:

ACCOUNTING Christopher Nobes
ADOLESCENCE Peter K. Smith
ADVERTISING Winston Fletcher
AFRICAN AMERICAN RELIGION
    Eddie S. Glaude Jr
AFRICAN HISTORY John Parker and
    Richard Rathbone
AFRICAN RELIGIONS Jacob K. Olupona
AGEING Nancy A. Pachana
AGNOSTICISM Robin Le Poidevin
AGRICULTURE Paul Brassley
    and Richard Soffe
ALEXANDER THE GREAT
    Hugh Bowden
ALGEBRA Peter M. Higgins
AMERICAN HISTORY Paul S. Boyer
AMERICAN IMMIGRATION
    David A. Gerber
AMERICAN LEGAL HISTORY
    G. Edward White
AMERICAN POLITICAL HISTORY
    Donald Critchlow
AMERICAN POLITICAL PARTIES
    AND ELECTIONS L. Sandy Maisel
AMERICAN POLITICS Richard M. Valelly
THE AMERICAN PRESIDENCY
    Charles O. Jones
THE AMERICAN REVOLUTION
    Robert J. Allison
AMERICAN SLAVERY
    Heather Andrea Williams
THE AMERICAN WEST Stephen Aron
AMERICAN WOMEN'S HISTORY
    Susan Ware

ANAESTHESIA Aidan O'Donnell
ANARCHISM Colin Ward
ANCIENT ASSYRIA Karen Radner
ANCIENT EGYPT Ian Shaw
ANCIENT EGYPTIAN ART AND
    ARCHITECTURE Christina Riggs
ANCIENT GREECE Paul Cartledge
THE ANCIENT NEAR EAST
    Amanda H. Podany
ANCIENT PHILOSOPHY Julia Annas
ANCIENT WARFARE Harry Sidebottom
ANGELS David Albert Jones
ANGLICANISM Mark Chapman
THE ANGLO-SAXON AGE John Blair
THE ANIMAL KINGDOM Peter Holland
ANIMAL RIGHTS David DeGrazia
THE ANTARCTIC Klaus Dodds
ANTISEMITISM Steven Beller
ANXIETY Daniel Freeman
    and Jason Freeman
THE APOCRYPHAL GOSPELS
    Paul Foster
ARCHAEOLOGY Paul Bahn
ARCHITECTURE Andrew Ballantyne
ARISTOCRACY William Doyle
ARISTOTLE Jonathan Barnes
ART HISTORY Dana Arnold
ART THEORY Cynthia Freeland
ASIAN AMERICAN HISTORY
    Madeline Y. Hsu
ASTROBIOLOGY David C. Catling
ASTROPHYSICS James Binney
ATHEISM Julian Baggini
AUGUSTINE Henry Chadwick

AUSTRALIA Kenneth Morgan
AUTISM Uta Frith
THE AVANT GARDE David Cottington
THE AZTECS David Carrasco
BABYLONIA Trevor Bryce
BACTERIA Sebastian G. B. Amyes
BARTHES Jonathan Culler
THE BEATS David Sterritt
BEAUTY Roger Scruton
BESTSELLERS John Sutherland
THE BIBLE John Riches
BIBLICAL ARCHAEOLOGY
    Eric H. Cline
BIOGRAPHY Hermione Lee
BLACK HOLES Katherine Blundell
BLOOD Chris Cooper
THE BLUES Elijah Wald
THE BODY Chris Shilling
THE BOOK OF MORMON
    Terryl Givens
BORDERS Alexander C. Diener
    and Joshua Hagen
THE BRAIN Michael O'Shea
THE BRICS Andrew F. Cooper
THE BRITISH CONSTITUTION
    Martin Loughlin
THE BRITISH EMPIRE Ashley Jackson
BRITISH POLITICS Anthony Wright
BUDDHA Michael Carrithers
BUDDHISM Damien Keown
BUDDHIST ETHICS Damien Keown
BYZANTIUM Peter Sarris
CANCER Nicholas James
CAPITALISM James Fulcher
CATHOLICISM Gerald O'Collins
CAUSATION Stephen Mumford
    and Rani Lill Anjum
THE CELL Terence Allen
    and Graham Cowling
THE CELTS Barry Cunliffe
CHAOS Leonard Smith
CHEMISTRY Peter Atkins
CHILD PSYCHOLOGY Usha Goswami
CHILDREN'S LITERATURE
    Kimberley Reynolds
CHINESE LITERATURE Sabina Knight
CHOICE THEORY Michael Allingham
CHRISTIAN ART Beth Williamson
CHRISTIAN ETHICS D. Stephen Long
CHRISTIANITY Linda Woodhead

CITIZENSHIP Richard Bellamy
CIVIL ENGINEERING
    David Muir Wood
CLASSICAL LITERATURE William Allan
CLASSICAL MYTHOLOGY
    Helen Morales
CLASSICS Mary Beard and
    John Henderson
CLAUSEWITZ Michael Howard
CLIMATE Mark Maslin
CLIMATE CHANGE Mark Maslin
COGNITIVE NEUROSCIENCE
    Richard Passingham
THE COLD WAR Robert McMahon
COLONIAL AMERICA Alan Taylor
COLONIAL LATIN AMERICAN
    LITERATURE Rolena Adorno
COMBINATORICS Robin Wilson
COMEDY Matthew Bevis
COMMUNISM Leslie Holmes
COMPLEXITY John H. Holland
THE COMPUTER Darrel Ince
COMPUTER SCIENCE
    Subrata Dasgupta
CONFUCIANISM Daniel K. Gardner
THE CONQUISTADORS
    Matthew Restall and
    Felipe Fernández-Armesto
CONSCIENCE Paul Strohm
CONSCIOUSNESS Susan Blackmore
CONTEMPORARY ART
    Julian Stallabrass
CONTEMPORARY FICTION
    Robert Eaglestone
CONTINENTAL PHILOSOPHY
    Simon Critchley
COPERNICUS Owen Gingerich
CORAL REEFS Charles Sheppard
CORPORATE SOCIAL RESPONSIBILITY
    Jeremy Moon
CORRUPTION Leslie Holmes
COSMOLOGY Peter Coles
CRIME FICTION Richard Bradford
CRIMINAL JUSTICE Julian V. Roberts
CRITICAL THEORY
    Stephen Eric Bronner
THE CRUSADES Christopher Tyerman
CRYPTOGRAPHY Fred Piper and
    Sean Murphy
CRYSTALLOGRAPHY A. M. Glazer

THE CULTURAL REVOLUTION
    Richard Curt Kraus
DADA AND SURREALISM
    David Hopkins
DANTE Peter Hainsworth
    and David Robey
DARWIN Jonathan Howard
THE DEAD SEA SCROLLS Timothy Lim
DECOLONIZATION Dane Kennedy
DEMOCRACY Bernard Crick
DERRIDA Simon Glendinning
DESCARTES Tom Sorell
DESERTS Nick Middleton
DESIGN John Heskett
DEVELOPMENTAL BIOLOGY
    Lewis Wolpert
THE DEVIL Darren Oldridge
DIASPORA Kevin Kenny
DICTIONARIES Lynda Mugglestone
DINOSAURS David Norman
DIPLOMACY Joseph M. Siracusa
DOCUMENTARY FILM
    Patricia Aufderheide
DREAMING J. Allan Hobson
DRUGS Les Iversen
DRUIDS Barry Cunliffe
EARLY MUSIC Thomas Forrest Kelly
THE EARTH Martin Redfern
EARTH SYSTEM SCIENCE Tim Lenton
ECONOMICS Partha Dasgupta
EDUCATION Gary Thomas
EGYPTIAN MYTH Geraldine Pinch
EIGHTEENTH-CENTURY BRITAIN
    Paul Langford
THE ELEMENTS Philip Ball
EMOTION Dylan Evans
EMPIRE Stephen Howe
ENGELS Terrell Carver
ENGINEERING David Blockley
ENGLISH LITERATURE Jonathan Bate
THE ENLIGHTENMENT
    John Robertson
ENTREPRENEURSHIP
    Paul Westhead and Mike Wright
ENVIRONMENTAL ECONOMICS
    Stephen Smith
ENVIRONMENTAL POLITICS
    Andrew Dobson
EPICUREANISM Catherine Wilson
EPIDEMIOLOGY Rodolfo Saracci

ETHICS Simon Blackburn
ETHNOMUSICOLOGY Timothy Rice
THE ETRUSCANS Christopher Smith
EUGENICS Philippa Levine
THE EUROPEAN UNION
    John Pinder and Simon Usherwood
EVOLUTION Brian and
    Deborah Charlesworth
EXISTENTIALISM Thomas Flynn
EXPLORATION Stewart A. Weaver
THE EYE Michael Land
FAMILY LAW Jonathan Herring
FASCISM Kevin Passmore
FASHION Rebecca Arnold
FEMINISM Margaret Walters
FILM Michael Wood
FILM MUSIC Kathryn Kalinak
THE FIRST WORLD WAR
    Michael Howard
FOLK MUSIC Mark Slobin
FOOD John Krebs
FORENSIC PSYCHOLOGY
    David Canter
FORENSIC SCIENCE Jim Fraser
FORESTS Jaboury Ghazoul
FOSSILS Keith Thomson
FOUCAULT Gary Gutting
THE FOUNDING FATHERS
    R. B. Bernstein
FRACTALS Kenneth Falconer
FREE SPEECH Nigel Warburton
FREE WILL Thomas Pink
FRENCH LITERATURE John D. Lyons
THE FRENCH REVOLUTION
    William Doyle
FREUD Anthony Storr
FUNDAMENTALISM Malise Ruthven
FUNGI Nicholas P. Money
GALAXIES John Gribbin
GALILEO Stillman Drake
GAME THEORY Ken Binmore
GANDHI Bhikhu Parekh
GENES Jonathan Slack
GENIUS Andrew Robinson
GEOGRAPHY John Matthews and
    David Herbert
GEOPOLITICS Klaus Dodds
GERMAN LITERATURE Nicholas Boyle
GERMAN PHILOSOPHY
    Andrew Bowie

GLOBAL CATASTROPHES Bill McGuire
GLOBAL ECONOMIC HISTORY
    Robert C. Allen
GLOBALIZATION Manfred Steger
GOD John Bowker
GOETHE Ritchie Robertson
THE GOTHIC Nick Groom
GOVERNANCE Mark Bevir
THE GREAT DEPRESSION AND THE
    NEW DEAL Eric Rauchway
HABERMAS James Gordon Finlayson
HAPPINESS Daniel M. Haybron
THE HARLEM RENAISSANCE
    Cheryl A. Wall
THE HEBREW BIBLE AS LITERATURE
    Tod Linafelt
HEGEL Peter Singer
HEIDEGGER Michael Inwood
HERMENEUTICS Jens Zimmermann
HERODOTUS Jennifer T. Roberts
HIEROGLYPHS Penelope Wilson
HINDUISM Kim Knott
HISTORY John H. Arnold
THE HISTORY OF ASTRONOMY
    Michael Hoskin
THE HISTORY OF CHEMISTRY
    William H. Brock
THE HISTORY OF LIFE
    Michael Benton
THE HISTORY OF MATHEMATICS
    Jacqueline Stedall
THE HISTORY OF MEDICINE
    William Bynum
THE HISTORY OF TIME
    Leofranc Holford-Strevens
HIV AND AIDS Alan Whiteside
HOBBES Richard Tuck
HOLLYWOOD Peter Decherney
HORMONES Martin Luck
HUMAN ANATOMY
    Leslie Klenerman
HUMAN EVOLUTION Bernard Wood
HUMAN RIGHTS Andrew Clapham
HUMANISM Stephen Law
HUME A. J. Ayer
HUMOUR Noël Carroll
THE ICE AGE Jamie Woodward
IDEOLOGY Michael Freeden
INDIAN CINEMA
    Ashish Rajadhyaksha
INDIAN PHILOSOPHY Sue Hamilton
INFECTIOUS DISEASE Marta L. Wayne
    and Benjamin M. Bolker
INFORMATION Luciano Floridi
INNOVATION Mark Dodgson and
    David Gann
INTELLIGENCE Ian J. Deary
INTERNATIONAL LAW
    Vaughan Lowe
INTERNATIONAL MIGRATION
    Khalid Koser
INTERNATIONAL RELATIONS
    Paul Wilkinson
INTERNATIONAL SECURITY
    Christopher S. Browning
IRAN Ali M. Ansari
ISLAM Malise Ruthven
ISLAMIC HISTORY Adam Silverstein
ISOTOPES Rob Ellam
ITALIAN LITERATURE
    Peter Hainsworth and David Robey
JESUS Richard Bauckham
JOURNALISM Ian Hargreaves
JUDAISM Norman Solomon
JUNG Anthony Stevens
KABBALAH Joseph Dan
KAFKA Ritchie Robertson
KANT Roger Scruton
KEYNES Robert Skidelsky
KIERKEGAARD Patrick Gardiner
KNOWLEDGE Jennifer Nagel
THE KORAN Michael Cook
LANDSCAPE ARCHITECTURE
    Ian H. Thompson
LANDSCAPES AND
    GEOMORPHOLOGY
    Andrew Goudie and Heather Viles
LANGUAGES Stephen R. Anderson
LATE ANTIQUITY Gillian Clark
LAW Raymond Wacks
THE LAWS OF THERMODYNAMICS
    Peter Atkins
LEADERSHIP Keith Grint
LEARNING Mark Haselgrove
LEIBNIZ Maria Rosa Antognazza
LIBERALISM Michael Freeden
LIGHT Ian Walmsley
LINCOLN Allen C. Guelzo
LINGUISTICS Peter Matthews
LITERARY THEORY Jonathan Culler

LOCKE John Dunn
LOGIC Graham Priest
LOVE Ronald de Sousa
MACHIAVELLI Quentin Skinner
MADNESS Andrew Scull
MAGIC Owen Davies
MAGNA CARTA Nicholas Vincent
MAGNETISM Stephen Blundell
MALTHUS Donald Winch
MANAGEMENT John Hendry
MAO Delia Davin
MARINE BIOLOGY Philip V. Mladenov
THE MARQUIS DE SADE John Phillips
MARTIN LUTHER Scott H. Hendrix
MARTYRDOM Jolyon Mitchell
MARX Peter Singer
MATERIALS Christopher Hall
MATHEMATICS Timothy Gowers
THE MEANING OF LIFE Terry Eagleton
MEASUREMENT David Hand
MEDICAL ETHICS Tony Hope
MEDICAL LAW Charles Foster
MEDIEVAL BRITAIN John Gillingham
   and Ralph A. Griffiths
MEDIEVAL LITERATURE
   Elaine Treharne
MEDIEVAL PHILOSOPHY
   John Marenbon
MEMORY Jonathan K. Foster
METAPHYSICS Stephen Mumford
THE MEXICAN REVOLUTION
   Alan Knight
MICHAEL FARADAY
   Frank A. J. L. James
MICROBIOLOGY Nicholas P. Money
MICROECONOMICS Avinash Dixit
MICROSCOPY Terence Allen
THE MIDDLE AGES Miri Rubin
MILITARY JUSTICE Eugene R. Fidell
MINERALS David Vaughan
MODERN ART David Cottington
MODERN CHINA Rana Mitter
MODERN DRAMA
   Kirsten E. Shepherd-Barr
MODERN FRANCE
   Vanessa R. Schwartz
MODERN IRELAND Senia Pašeta
MODERN ITALY Anna Cento Bull
MODERN JAPAN
   Christopher Goto-Jones

MODERN LATIN AMERICAN
   LITERATURE
   Roberto González Echevarría
MODERN WAR Richard English
MODERNISM Christopher Butler
MOLECULAR BIOLOGY
   Aysha Divan and Janice A. Royds
MOLECULES Philip Ball
THE MONGOLS Morris Rossabi
MOONS David A. Rothery
MORMONISM
   Richard Lyman Bushman
MOUNTAINS Martin F. Price
MUHAMMAD Jonathan A. C. Brown
MULTICULTURALISM Ali Rattansi
MUSIC Nicholas Cook
MYTH Robert A. Segal
THE NAPOLEONIC WARS
   Mike Rapport
NATIONALISM Steven Grosby
NELSON MANDELA Elleke Boehmer
NEOLIBERALISM Manfred Steger and
   Ravi Roy
NETWORKS Guido Caldarelli and
   Michele Catanzaro
THE NEW TESTAMENT
   Luke Timothy Johnson
THE NEW TESTAMENT AS
   LITERATURE Kyle Keefer
NEWTON Robert Iliffe
NIETZSCHE Michael Tanner
NINETEENTH-CENTURY
   BRITAIN Christopher Harvie and
   H. C. G. Matthew
THE NORMAN CONQUEST
   George Garnett
NORTH AMERICAN INDIANS
   Theda Perdue and Michael D. Green
NORTHERN IRELAND
   Marc Mulholland
NOTHING Frank Close
NUCLEAR PHYSICS Frank Close
NUCLEAR POWER Maxwell Irvine
NUCLEAR WEAPONS
   Joseph M. Siracusa
NUMBERS Peter M. Higgins
NUTRITION David A. Bender
OBJECTIVITY Stephen Gaukroger
THE OLD TESTAMENT
   Michael D. Coogan

THE ORCHESTRA D. Kern Holoman
ORGANIZATIONS Mary Jo Hatch
PANDEMICS Christian W. McMillen
PAGANISM Owen Davies
THE PALESTINIAN-ISRAELI
    CONFLICT Martin Bunton
PARTICLE PHYSICS Frank Close
PAUL E. P. Sanders
PEACE Oliver P. Richmond
PENTECOSTALISM William K. Kay
THE PERIODIC TABLE Eric R. Scerri
PHILOSOPHY Edward Craig
PHILOSOPHY IN THE ISLAMIC
    WORLD Peter Adamson
PHILOSOPHY OF LAW
    Raymond Wacks
PHILOSOPHY OF SCIENCE
    Samir Okasha
PHOTOGRAPHY Steve Edwards
PHYSICAL CHEMISTRY Peter Atkins
PILGRIMAGE Ian Reader
PLAGUE Paul Slack
PLANETS David A. Rothery
PLANTS Timothy Walker
PLATE TECTONICS Peter Molnar
PLATO Julia Annas
POLITICAL PHILOSOPHY David Miller
POLITICS Kenneth Minogue
POSTCOLONIALISM Robert Young
POSTMODERNISM Christopher Butler
POSTSTRUCTURALISM
    Catherine Belsey
PREHISTORY Chris Gosden
PRESOCRATIC PHILOSOPHY
    Catherine Osborne
PRIVACY Raymond Wacks
PROBABILITY John Haigh
PROGRESSIVISM Walter Nugent
PROTESTANTISM Mark A. Noll
PSYCHIATRY Tom Burns
PSYCHOANALYSIS Daniel Pick
PSYCHOLOGY Gillian Butler and
    Freda McManus
PSYCHOTHERAPY Tom Burns and
    Eva Burns-Lundgren
PUBLIC ADMINISTRATION
    Stella Z. Theodoulou and Ravi K. Roy
PUBLIC HEALTH Virginia Berridge
PURITANISM Francis J. Bremer
THE QUAKERS Pink Dandelion

QUANTUM THEORY
    John Polkinghorne
RACISM Ali Rattansi
RADIOACTIVITY Claudio Tuniz
RASTAFARI Ennis B. Edmonds
THE REAGAN REVOLUTION
    Gil Troy
REALITY Jan Westerhoff
THE REFORMATION Peter Marshall
RELATIVITY Russell Stannard
RELIGION IN AMERICA Timothy Beal
THE RENAISSANCE Jerry Brotton
RENAISSANCE ART
    Geraldine A. Johnson
REVOLUTIONS Jack A. Goldstone
RHETORIC Richard Toye
RISK Baruch Fischhoff and John Kadvany
RITUAL Barry Stephenson
RIVERS Nick Middleton
ROBOTICS Alan Winfield
ROMAN BRITAIN Peter Salway
THE ROMAN EMPIRE
    Christopher Kelly
THE ROMAN REPUBLIC
    David M. Gwynn
ROMANTICISM Michael Ferber
ROUSSEAU Robert Wokler
RUSSELL A. C. Grayling
RUSSIAN HISTORY Geoffrey Hosking
RUSSIAN LITERATURE Catriona Kelly
THE RUSSIAN REVOLUTION
    S. A. Smith
SAVANNAS Peter A. Furley
SCHIZOPHRENIA Chris Frith and
    Eve Johnstone
SCHOPENHAUER Christopher Janaway
SCIENCE AND RELIGION
    Thomas Dixon
SCIENCE FICTION David Seed
THE SCIENTIFIC REVOLUTION
    Lawrence M. Principe
SCOTLAND Rab Houston
SEXUALITY Véronique Mottier
SHAKESPEARE'S COMEDIES
    Bart van Es
SIKHISM Eleanor Nesbitt
THE SILK ROAD James A. Millward
SLANG Jonathon Green
SLEEP Steven W. Lockley and
    Russell G. Foster

SOCIAL AND CULTURAL
  ANTHROPOLOGY
  John Monaghan and Peter Just
SOCIAL PSYCHOLOGY Richard J. Crisp
SOCIAL WORK Sally Holland and
  Jonathan Scourfield
SOCIALISM Michael Newman
SOCIOLINGUISTICS John Edwards
SOCIOLOGY Steve Bruce
SOCRATES C. C. W. Taylor
SOUND Mike Goldsmith
THE SOVIET UNION Stephen Lovell
THE SPANISH CIVIL WAR
  Helen Graham
SPANISH LITERATURE Jo Labanyi
SPINOZA Roger Scruton
SPIRITUALITY Philip Sheldrake
SPORT Mike Cronin
STARS Andrew King
STATISTICS David J. Hand
STEM CELLS Jonathan Slack
STRUCTURAL ENGINEERING
  David Blockley
STUART BRITAIN John Morrill
SUPERCONDUCTIVITY
  Stephen Blundell
SYMMETRY Ian Stewart
TAXATION Stephen Smith
TEETH Peter S. Ungar
TERRORISM Charles Townshend
THEATRE Marvin Carlson
THEOLOGY David F. Ford
THOMAS AQUINAS Fergus Kerr
THOUGHT Tim Bayne

TIBETAN BUDDHISM
  Matthew T. Kapstein
TOCQUEVILLE Harvey C. Mansfield
TRAGEDY Adrian Poole
TRANSLATION Matthew Reynolds
THE TROJAN WAR Eric H. Cline
TRUST Katherine Hawley
THE TUDORS John Guy
TWENTIETH-CENTURY BRITAIN
  Kenneth O. Morgan
THE UNITED NATIONS
  Jussi M. Hanhimäki
THE U.S. CONGRESS Donald A. Ritchie
THE U.S. SUPREME COURT
  Linda Greenhouse
UTOPIANISM Lyman Tower Sargent
THE VIKINGS Julian Richards
VIRUSES Dorothy H. Crawford
WAR AND TECHNOLOGY
  Alex Roland
WATER John Finney
THE WELFARE STATE David Garland
WILLIAM SHAKESPEARE
  Stanley Wells
WITCHCRAFT Malcolm Gaskill
WITTGENSTEIN A. C. Grayling
WORK Stephen Fineman
WORLD MUSIC Philip Bohlman
THE WORLD TRADE
  ORGANIZATION Amrita Narlikar
WORLD WAR II Gerhard L. Weinberg
WRITING AND SCRIPT
  Andrew Robinson
ZIONISM Michael Stanislawski

Available soon:

TELESCOPES Geoff Cottrell
CALVINISM Jon Balserak
HOME Michael Allen Fox

ROCKS Jan Zalasiewicz
BANKING John Goddard and
  John O. S. Wilson

For more information visit our website

www.oup.com/vsi/

Madeline Y. Hsu

ASIAN AMERICAN HISTORY

A Very Short Introduction

OXFORD
UNIVERSITY PRESS

OXFORD
UNIVERSITY PRESS

Oxford University Press is a department of the University of Oxford.
It furthers the University's objective of excellence in research, scholarship,
and education by publishing worldwide. Oxford is a registered trade mark of
Oxford University Press in the UK and certain other countries.

Published in the United States of America by Oxford University Press
198 Madison Avenue, New York, NY 10016, United States of America.

Library of Congress Cataloging-in-Publication Data

Names: Hsu, Madeline Yuan-yin, author.
Title: Asian American history : a very short introduction / Madeline Y. Hsu.
Description: New York City : Oxford University Press, [2017] |
Series: Very short introductions | Includes
bibliographical references and index.
Identifiers: LCCN 2016028406| ISBN 9780190219765 (pbk.) |
ISBN 9780190219789 (ebook epub) | ISBN 9780190219796 (online resource)
Subjects: LCSH: Asian Americans—History. | Asian Americans—
Social conditions. | Asian Americans—Cultural assimilation. |
United States—Race relations—History.
Classification: LCC E184.A75 H89 2016 | DDC 973/.0495—dc23 LC record
available at https://lccn.loc.gov/2016028406

Printed and bound by
CPI Group (UK) Ltd, Croydon, CR0 4YY

Contents

List of illustrations xiii

Acknowledgments xv

Preface: An orientation xvii

1 Empires and migration 1

2 Race and the American republic 25

3 Living in the margins 52

4 Crucibles of war 83

5 Imperialism, immigration, and capitalism 116

References 147

Further reading 151

Index 155

List of illustrations

1   Late-Ming plate for Mexican
    or Spanish markets, between
    1590 and 1620 **3**
    Peabody Essex Museum AE85571

2   Trade routes linking Asia to
    the Americas **15**

3   "The Chinese must go" **28**
    Harper's Weekly, September 13,
    1879. Library of Congress LOT 14012,
    no. 336

4   The 1917 Barred Zone **42**

5   Young Filipino men, Seattle,
    about 1935 **66**
    University of Washington Libraries,
    Special Collections, SOC1037

6   San Francisco Chinatown's
    Grant Avenue **71**
    Author's collection

7   Mine Okubo, *Waiting in Line
    to Receive Vaccinations*,
    Tanforan Assembly Center, San
    Bruno, California, 1942 **85**
    Japanese American National Museum
    (Gift of Mine Okubo Estate, 2007.62)

8   Chinese American women for
    Lyndon Baines Johnson, San
    Francisco, 1964 **108**
    Courtesy of the Asian American Studies
    Collections, Ethnic Studies Library,
    University of California, Berkeley

9   Chinatown gates, Austin,
    Texas **127**
    Photo by author

10 Indian owners of the Budget
    Motel, Wichita, Kansas posing
    for "The Arch Motel
    Project" **136**
    Art director *Pardon My Hindi/
    Chiraag Bhakta; photo by Mark
    Hewko

Acknowledgments

This book benefitted from the comments and insights of some valued colleagues, including Nancy Toff, the two anonymous readers, my colleagues Daina Berry and Sam Vong, and students from my spring 2015 graduate seminar, "Race and Migration": Christopher Babits, Sandy Chang, Eddie Hsu, David Hutchinson, Michel Lee, Noreen Naseem Rodriguez, Lauren Osmer, Leila Grace Pandy, Zach Schlachter, and Jing Zhai. I am also grateful for the capable contributions of project managers Elda Granata and Ethiraju Saraswathi and copyeditor Kristen Holt-Browning.

Preface: An orientation

Asian migrations to the Americas proceeded across several centuries of dramatic economic and political transformations. The expanding reach of European empires brought all parts of the world into increasingly regular contact through the unequal redistribution of technologies toward a number of ends: travel; political authority; economics and trade; the accumulation of profits and capital; and the dissemination of both belief systems, and knowledge about newly encountered societies and places. Perhaps the key movements were those of the people needed to manage and carry out these developments: sailors, explorers, merchants, bureaucrats, missionaries, and laborers under varying degrees of coercion. Often, but not always, the outlines of empires configured the routes of their journeys. Even as humans were becoming drastically more mobile in this emerging global order, increasingly influential nation-states sought to impose fixed boundaries and sovereignties onto geographic spaces, and to rigidly categorize different peoples into nationalities corresponding to differentiating hierarchies of biologically determined capacities marked by race.

As the merger of the Asian and American hemispheres intensified due to migration, such contradictions between the workings of empires and nations produced conflicts and exclusions. Even as Asians workers, entrepreneurs, and merchants helped to develop the riches of the American West through their sweat, ingenuity, and connections, they presented an unanticipated challenge to conceptions of equal citizenship in a nation premised on immigration. Perceived as issuing from essentially different, inferior, and therefore inassimilable, races and cultures, as compared to the predominantly white, Anglo-Saxon Protestants who had founded the American republic, Asians struggled to claim acceptance and equal opportunity in the United States. Racial segregation concerned not just African and Native Americans, but Asians as well, primarily in the arena of limiting immigration. As a primarily immigrant population, the presumed inassimilability of Asians justified the 180-degree about-face in national attitudes and policy, through which the United States began erecting its earliest actively enforced controls on immigration. The goal of Asian exclusion provided the ideological, legal, and institutional foundations for prevailing conditions of greatly diminished access to legal immigration, and the vastly expanded array of powers claimed by federal authorities over border matters and policing of unauthorized immigrants today.

Asians continued to immigrate despite these fortifying barriers, and managed to carve out lives and livelihoods across generations through perseverance and careful attention to opportunities and conditions in the United States. Their systematic strategizing— through the court system and political activism, for economic security and attainment—has contributed to the development of national standards which have led to the diminishing of racial discriminations on a host of fronts including citizenship, immigration rights, employment, property ownership, marriage, and access to social services. In claiming American lives, Asians have indelibly transformed the United States as well. In conjunction with the international pressures of World War II and the Cold War, civil rights activism forced the removal of overt racial and national-origins discrimination from laws restricting immigration and citizenship. The ensuing emphasis on employment preferences—which privilege "skilled" or knowledge workers—and family reunification have operated to position Asian Americans as a "model minority" that has gained acceptance, by virtue of overachievement in education, employment, and family stability as screened through immigration processes. As explored in this brief history, the stories and experiences of the predominantly immigrant population of Asian Americans reflect starkly the choices the United States has made about what kinds of people it is willing to welcome and to include as Americans— and those whom it rejects.

Despite the title of this volume, the category "Asian American" is a misnomer until we reach the late 1960s, when nativity and shared experience in the United States had finally produced a generation that found more in common through the country of their birth than the countries of their ancestors. Country of origin, marked by daily realities such as language, recreational and food preferences, family practices, economic conditions, political orientation, and religion, remains a key shaper of identity and community for the majority of Asians who are immigrants.

The category "Asian American" includes over forty different national and language groups from regions of the world extending from the Middle East, and reaching through India, the Southeast Asian peninsula and island archipelagoes, China, Korea, and Japan. Following Chinese and Japanese practice, surnames appear before given names. This volume synthesizes scholarship produced by many outstanding colleagues whose publications are cited more specifically in the reference and recommended reading sections. The brevity of the VSI format prohibits a fuller listing of major works. Any errors of fact or interpretation remain my responsibility.

Chapter 1
Empires and migration

Centuries before the Gold Rush, Asians began traveling to
America. On a stormy fall day in 1587, the Spanish galleon
Nuestra Senora de Esperanza found shelter in a cove now known
as Morro Bay, on the coast of California. Its captain, Pedro da
Unamuno, brought several Filipino "Luzon Indians" with him
onshore to help scout for materials to repair the damage inflicted
by the tumultuous seas encountered during their journey from
Manila. After some minor skirmishes with indigenous Native
Americans, da Unamuno proclaimed Spanish fealty over the area,
repaired the ship, and continued sailing south to his intended
destination of Acapulco, the eastern outpost of Spain's trans-
Pacific empire. The journey took advantage of trade winds and
ocean currents which could power enormous two-thousand-ton
galleons for five-thousand-mile voyages bearing goods such as
New World silver, Asian slaves, and Chinese teas and porcelain,
all of which would be traded in Manila. Despite the brevity of de
Unamuno's visit to North America, the trip serves nonetheless
to illustrate more general and long-term dynamics of Asian
migrations and encounters with the Western hemisphere. The
Luzon Indians' brief visit suggests the Pacific Ocean's role as a
conduit, rather than a barrier, to commercial, cultural, and political
relations; Western America as a site of opportunity for adventurous
Asians; and the many kinds of mobility fostered by colonial
empires whose global reach brought together all parts of the world.

Conquest and capitalism

Driven by tremendous greed and ambition, empire-builders developed the global organizations and networks, shipping and communications technologies, and huge reserves of capital needed to connect all parts of the world to Europe in the name of commerce and Christianity. By the late sixteenth century, such energies and drives had disciplined the vast, once unknown Pacific into an annual journey of six to eight months. Clipper ships reduced travel times even further and by the 1870s, steamships plied the route year-round in only three weeks. Imperially driven quests for profit and influence produced shipping routes linking trading centers around the world, which sought to secure investments and control. Alongside commodities and agents of empire such as missionaries, government bureaucrats, traders, bankers, soldiers, sailors, clerks, and teachers, Asian peoples migrated as well.

The "Luzon Indians" who accompanied da Unamuno illustrate how this dispersal followed the expanding linkages forged by European empires. Imperial quests for economic growth generated increased appetites for workers, many of whom were Asians, to provide the grueling labor needed for profit-making ventures such as plantations, construction of roads and railroads, guano-gathering, mining, lumbering, fishing, canneries, and sailing ships. We cannot know if the "Luzon Indians" had joined da Unamuno's ship willingly or by some form of coercion or trickery, but they were plausibly the first Asians to set foot on the North American continent in the early modern era, conveyed by this confluence of expanding maritime empires and intensifying economic development of the New World. Under their own agency, Asians made use of these circuits and the accompanying, expanding array of economic opportunities to seek fortunes on their own terms as merchants, students, skilled workers, brokers, laborers, entrepreneurs of every sort, sailors, soldiers, and adventurers. Their presence in North America increased and became ever more inevitable with the intensifying linkages between the two continents. This entwinement began with the galleon trade in 1565, when Spain claimed its largest Asian colony in the Philippines and proceeded to connect the ends of its empire in annual voyages that persisted until 1815, as Mexico struggled to break away from its empire.

These emerging networks explain the singular life of Catarina de San Juan, a slave captured from her home on the west coast of India by Portuguese slavers around 1610. A competitor with Spain for advantage in maritime trade, Portugal focused on economic

1. This late-Ming dynasty plate bears the symbol of the Order of St. Augustine—a double-headed eagle over a pierced heart—and was manufactured for either Mexican or Spanish markets between 1590 and 1620. This blue-and-white porcelain was produced in the famous Jingdezhen factories, which were active in the export trade.

activities in coastal areas, as tracked through Catarina's protracted journey to the Americas. Her captors brought her to the port of Cochin, where she was most likely baptized and renamed, then around the Indian subcontinent and across the Bay of Bengal, through the Straits of Malacca, and up the South China Sea to Manila in the Philippines, which was a major slave-trading center serving the full reaches of the Spanish Empire during the seventeenth century. Catarina was sold at the slave market alongside slaves brought from Japan; sub-Saharan Africa; Muslim areas in the southern Philippines; the Indonesian islands of Borneo, Java, and Maluku; Bengal including parts of Bangladesh and India; Sri Lanka; Macau; Timor; Melaka; and Malay. Her eventual owner in Puebla, Mexico had delegated representatives to purchase a household slave for him in Manila. *"Chinos"* (slaves from Asia) were valued as domestic servants in part because they were perceived as more acculturated after extensive exposure and training in Portuguese, and later Spanish, households in the Philippines during years of waiting for the long voyages that brought them to Mexico. Catarina, for example, had quickly embraced Christianity and adopted ascetic practices.

After she was purchased, Catarina traveled via a Manila Galleon and arrived in Acapulco in 1619, walking the arduous China Road (*via de china*) inland to Mexico City and then to Puebla. Only five years later, she was manumitted, out of respect for her religiosity. She remained in Puebla working as a servant, using her earnings to free other slaves, and gathering a devout following until her death in 1688, after which local residents sought to have her beatified in recognition of her celebrated status as a lay religious woman (*beata*). (In contrast, her contemporary religious devotee, Juana Esperanze de San Alberto, was not nominated for sainthood. Although equally famed for her piety, Juana was of African ancestry, which was seen as a nearly insurmountable barrier to sainthood.) Despite the difficult circumstances of her coming to the Americas, Catarina adapted well to become an exemplary subject of the Spanish Empire's outpost in Mexico.

4

By the late seventeenth century, the Church had facilitated the end of the Spanish Empire's trade in *chino* slaves by categorizing them as indigenous vassals who required imperial protections from slavery. In contrast, the trade in African slaves continued for two more centuries. Although the total number of Asian slaves who ended up in Mexico is unknown, other early Asian arrivals also left traces. In 1635, irate local barbers in Mexico City filed a court complaint alleging unfair competition from Chinese. In 1883, the traveler and journalist Lafcadio Hearn described St. Malo, a Filipino settlement in the bayous south of New Orleans, which he claimed dated back fifty years. Residents asserted that their village had been founded by sailors known as "Manila Men," who had deserted from the dire conditions onboard Spanish ships. According to oral accounts from the 1930s, several generations of their descendants had resided in shrimping villages, such as Manila Village in Jefferson Parish, up to the 1880s. Speakers of Tagalog and Cebuano intermarried with local women and became part of local lore, although the physical traces of these villages have long since disappeared.

Colonization and adaptation

By the eighteenth century, more recently emerging imperial powers were in the process of displacing the Spanish and Portuguese from their territories. Latecomers to empire, particularly the British and French, sought profits not only through trade but also by developing production of commodities such as metals, tobacco, sugar, rubber, and cotton. The transformation of native environments into regulated plantations and mines required millions of laborers and more extensive political control of Asian colonies, an intensification of colonial interference that fostered higher levels of migration to North America.

England's emergence as a maritime power challenged the dominance of Spain, Portugal, and Holland, with its 1588 defeat of the mighty Spanish Armada marking its steady ascent and eventual assumption of leadership in trade of the most desired goods in the form of Chinese silks, porcelains, lacquerware, and after the 1660s, tea. Status in colonial America was conveyed by possession of such prized goods, and the enormous profits to be gained motivated the British to ban Americans from directly trading with China—a source of such anger that, in their challenge for independence, American colonists protested by dumping English stores of Asian tea into Boston harbor in 1773. One of the first acts taken by independent American businessmen was to dispatch the clipper ship *Empress of China* in 1784 on the fourteen-month journey from New York to Guangzhou east across the Atlantic and through the Indian Ocean, a venture so profitable that its investors were wealthy for generations. As an independent nation, the United States joined the general race for trading riches from Asia, its competitive edge shifting and growing as its territorial empire expanded westward to incorporate the Pacific Ocean's eastern rim.

Until the United States realized the full potential of its Pacific destiny during World War II, the British Empire remained the most extensive world power, in no small part through the prowess of naval talent such as Captain James Cook, who explored and mapped much of the Caribbean and Pacific realms. Although he failed to find the fabled Northwest Passage, he captained the *Resolution* and *Discovery* to Hawaii on January 18, 1778; this armed arrival forced Hawaiians to rapidly adjust to the growing presence and demands of outsiders determined to impose control on their persons and territory with the goal of maximizing profits. The steady ascendance of American influence over Hawaii provides a model of how foreign business interests, backed by the military power of their imperial states, subjugated indigenous political and social structures while claiming land and resources to develop for maximum profitability. The banners of progress and Christianity were used to justify such forceful conquests, based on the view of indigenous peoples as savages and heathens whose lower position in racial hierarchies required intervention by more civilized—and lighter-skinned—colonizers. Amid these adverse circumstances, Hawaii's leaders sought to adapt to their unsought entanglement in global transfers of trade, status, and authority.

The irresistible interaction with Westerners imposed by Cook led the Hawaiian King Kamehameha to decide that to protect his kingdom, he had to send his twelve-year-old son to learn from the more powerful societies battering at his doors. He appointed two young men, Thomas Hopu and 'Opukaha'ia, to accompany the prince on an American ship captained by Caleb Brintnall of New England. Brintnall sailed first to the Pacific Northwest to pick up fur pelts for exchange in the China trade, but by the time the ship stopped back at Hawaii, King Kamehameha had changed his mind and retrieved his son. Hopu and 'Opukaha'ia, however, decided to keep traveling and worked onboard ship to pay for their way to China and points further west. The ship stayed six months in Macao and Guangzhou before continuing, heavily laden with trade goods, to cross the Indian Ocean, around the Cape of Good Hope, then across the Atlantic to arrive in New York in the fall of 1809. The young Hawaiians readily found a series of local sponsors who provided housing and education, particularly for 'Opukaha'ia, who had converted to Christianity and decided to become a missionary. In 1817, they began studying at the American Board of Commissioners' Foreign Mission School in Cornwall, Connecticut, which aimed to train missionaries for international service: in 1825, it enrolled not only Hawaiians, but also Chinese, Native Indians, a Portuguese from Azores, and a "Jew from England."

Although the promising 'Opukaha'ia died before returning home, Hopu accompanied the first group of missionaries stationed in Hawaii, for whom he worked as an interpreter. Hopu would end his days in the Hawaiian islands after making another venture to the gold country of California. His quest for education—driven by hopes of acquiring and adapting from more powerful, Western nations modes of learning, social and political systems, science and math, and technology to rejuvenate and strengthen their weakened homeland states—presaged the motivations of generations of future Asian youths who would also venture to America.

In return, missionaries hoping to save heathen souls were always at the forefront of Westerners seeking to reshape Asian and Pacific Islander societies based on the abiding belief in the superiority of their own Western civilization. They propelled significant transformations, although not always on spiritual planes. Starting in the 1820s, successive waves of New England missionaries became the founders of Hawaii's plantation society and promoters of its eventual absorption as a US territory. They attained tremendous wealth by engineering the conversion of Hawaii from a society of fishermen and small cultivators divided into tribes and ruled by chiefs and kings, into an industrialized agricultural economy generating wealth through cattle-ranching, sugar, pineapples, and coffee. Hawaii became the latest addition to the globally expanding "plantation complex" developed to produce the endlessly popular commodity of sugar.

Large-scale agriculture as a form of colonial development had reached from the Portuguese island of Madeira to Brazil, then from the eastern Caribbean to Saint Domingue and Jamaica after 1700; and then to Cuba, Mauritius, Peru, Fiji, and Hawaii during the 1830s. Massive plantations cleared then flattened landscapes to concentrate agricultural output into cash crops which served as the new focus for employment and commercial options, while generating enormous demands for workers. After exhausting the supply of locals, the plantation system sought workers from all corners of the world who arrived under varying degrees of coercion including slavery, indentured status, and limited term contracts. Industrial agriculture, or "factories in the fields," were powerful magnets that simultaneously increased and diversified local populations by drawing hundreds of thousands of migrants from Asia as workers—as well as merchants, brokers, artisans, relatives, and service providers, who formed into newly heterogeneous communities.

William Hooper of Ladd and Company established the first Hawaiian sugar plantation on Kauai in 1835, instituting far-reaching changes such as consolidating ownership of large tracts of land, bringing that land under mono-cultivation, building housing and workshops for plantation employees, and constructing a mill dam, sugar house, boiling house, and sugar mill. Hooper turned first to native Hawaiians as workers but almost immediately became dissatisfied. He found it hard to employ them in sufficient numbers—disease had decimated indigenous populations from 300,000 in 1780 to 70,000 in 1850—and he found them hard to discipline. By 1838, he started employing Chinese who were already resident on the islands. Despite such challenges, the Koloa Plantation produced 30 tons of sugar and 170 barrels of molasses by the time he left the next year.

Production kept growing as Americans kept arriving from the mainland and claiming more resources and influence. They formed the Royal Hawaiian Agricultural Society in 1850 and composed a powerful interest group that wrested land ownership away from Hawaiians and promoted regulations that favored their own economic interests over those of the indigenous populations. Hawaii fell deeper into the orbit of the United States, which reached the Pacific coast with the Gold Rush and the 1848 Treaty of Guadalupe Hidalgo, by which Mexico's northern districts, notably California, became American territory with a booming population and demand for Hawaiian products. As the United States pursued its manifest destiny in moving further westward, Hawaii's economy became increasingly reliant on the export of coffee, sugar, fruits, and vegetables to the mainland, with which it signed the 1875 Reciprocity Treaty abolishing duties on Hawaiian products and locking in the United States as its main market. By 1878, 90 percent of Hawaii's total exports went to the mainland, reaching 99 percent by 1899, consisting primarily of sugar.

Production output increased as well, creating growing demands for laborers. From 1875 to 1910, the plantation work force increased from 3,260 to 43,917 and the acres under cultivation grew from 12,000 to 214,000.

A Pacific nation

The Gold Rush hastened the United States' rush to grant statehood to California in 1850, leapfrogging from Missouri over the Great Plains and the Rocky Mountains in reaching the Pacific. Shipping routes adjusted accordingly as San Francisco paired with Hong Kong, Britain's newest colony in East Asia, to anchor either end of the circuit. Travel times between the United States and China diminished rapidly from the era when clippers sailed eastward toward Europe, around Africa and India, and through Southeast Asia in a journey of months. In the mid-nineteenth century, such journeys from New York to Shanghai required at least two and a half months, while the trip from Boston and New York (sailing around the Horn to reach San Francisco) took 115 days; the record of 89 days was set in 1851 by the clipper *Flying Cloud*. In contrast, most trans-Pacific voyages to Hong Kong took only 45 to 50 days, with the record set by the *Challenge* at 33 days in 1852. American trade ambitions shifted with the new possibilities offered by Pacific passages, and the first transoceanic shipping line was established in 1867, deploying both steam and sail tramp ships.

International travel grew cheaper and available at more ports, facilitating the rapid increase in Asian migrations over the nineteenth century. Economic incentives to migrate had grown as well, as intensifying development of colonial territories generated abundant employment and entrepreneurial opportunities in plantation agriculture, trade, shipping, mines, factories, lumber, fishing, services, and brokering of various kinds. The overall decline of indigenous populations in the New World and the 1807 British ban on the slave trade fuelled demands for new sources of workers, primarily from China and India, who made their way to the New World as part of emerging global diasporas.

These flows were significantly, but not entirely, shaped by transformations enacted under the duress of imperial aggressions. India's proximity and central trading location made it an early victim of European use of military force to impose control over commercial activities—a pattern of maritime violence pioneered by the explorer Vasco de Gama at the turn of the sixteenth century. Competing imperial powers on the Indian subcontinent transformed agricultural economies, undermined local handicrafts, and displaced populations, so that by the nineteenth century, Indians comprised one of the largest mobile populations in the world, with more than thirty million leaving colonial India between 1834 and 1930. Numbers surged in part as the decline of the African slave trade fuelled demands for alternative sources of laborers. As indentured workers, known as *kulis*, but also through recruitment and under direction from Indian migration brokers, about 90 percent journeyed westward across the Bay of Bengal to work in British colonial territories such as Malay and the Straits Settlement, Sri Lanka, and Burma. About two million went to British territories in the Caribbean, Pacific, and Indian Oceans. Around two million Punjabis journeyed as merchants, travelers, and soldiers throughout Southeast Asia and across the Indian Ocean through networks to Hong Kong, Macao, Shanghai, Singapore, and Manila, with about eighty thousand making their way beyond coastal Southeast Asian circuits to reach Canada, Australia, Hawaii, the United States, Mexico, Panama, and Argentina. Before the mid-twentieth century, however, relatively few Indians reached the Americas.

Chinese, primarily Cantonese from the Pearl River Delta region close to Hong Kong, were one of the first and largest Asian groups to migrate to North America, as a result of well-honed practices of migration and overseas trade, as well as China's relative proximity to California and the commanding allure of Chinese markets in motivating the imposition of trade relations. The first Opium War (1839–1842) broke open the great treasure chest of China, culminating centuries of increasing insistence that Chinese deal with Western merchants on their terms. In the 1790s, the British product of Indian-grown opium finally tipped the imbalance of trade in favor of Western merchants to further weaken a Chinese empire already in crisis. The outflow of silver produced steadily creeping inflation, which aggravated long-standing domestic conditions of overpopulation, agricultural shortfalls, widespread official corruption, an inefficient tax structure, and pervasive social unrest. The tripling of China's population over as many centuries had, by the 1740s, propelled growing numbers of workers, sailors, artisans, junk traders, and merchants to look abroad in search of opportunities generated by colonial development in Malaysia, Indonesia, Singapore, the Philippines and the independent monarchies of Burma, Thailand, Vietnam, Laos, and Cambodia. Chinese were valued as experienced business assets accustomed to the managing of labor, import-export trading, and accumulation of capital, despite occasional crackdowns stemming from anxieties about their growing economic clout. In the nineteenth century, Chinese ventured beyond Asia, including the few dozens who reached Hawaii and were available to work for Hooper on the Koloa Plantation.

After centuries of resisting European demands for more trade, China was forced to work with Western powers on their terms, with diplomatic "negotiations" stemming from lost military confrontations that produced economic agreements greatly favoring foreign, Western interests. Unable to defend against British warships, and later those of Americans, French, Italians, Belgians, Russians, and Germans, China signed a series of unequal treaties beginning with the 1842 Treaty of Nanjing, which ended the first Opium War. This was but the first of many conflicts deliberately started to provide conditions that would allow further Western demands—a pattern of ignominious military defeats followed by more unequal treaties conceding an expanding array of transgressions: treaty ports and territory, extraterritoriality and immunity to local laws, travel and residency rights, control over customs and taxes, and indemnities.

As its economy, urban and rural spaces, governance, and social organizations came under increasing exposure to Western interests, China entered its era of mass migration, in which 14.7 million departed between 1869 and 1939. The ruling Qing dynasty (1644–1911) had become so weak that not only could it not end the odious opium trade, it also could not prevent the coerced migration of Chinese through the "coolie" trade, which began as early as 1807. Until the practice was banned in 1874, up to tens of thousands of Chinese annually were coerced, through trickery, capture, and deceit, to labor under the destitute conditions on the plantations of Cuba, Guyana, and Trinidad and Tobago, and the guano fields of Peru. Although often compared to slavery with dire political implications for those so labelled, coolie systems of contract and indenture entailed ownership of labor but not of persons who could, if they survived the arduous conditions, regain control of their mobility and work.

Many more Chinese migrated as independent agents aided by merchants, brokers, labor recruiters, and others eager to profit by providing information about possible destinations, making travel arrangements, and offering credit. Hawaii illustrates some of these broader patterns of Asian migrations, with its driving demands for workers but also the ancillary opportunities for employment, entrepreneurship, and resettlement it provided. Its plantation class had quickly realized the limits of hiring workers locally and in 1850 founded the Royal Hawaiian Agricultural Society, which in 1852 had arranged for the first shipment of Chinese contract workers. Despite the great numbers available, Chinese were not entirely satisfactory as a labor force. Between 1852 and 1887, almost fifty thousand Chinese workers arrived but did not stay on the plantations. At the end of their contracts, most left, with 38 percent returning to China while others founded their own businesses or farms. Plantation owners also feared worker unrest. By the early 1880s, Chinese had become the dominant group of plantation workers. As recently as 1872, native Hawaiians had been 82.8 percent of the work force, with the 4,392 Chinese comprising only 11.5 percent. In 1882, however, Chinese ranks stood at 49.1 percent compared to only 25.1 percent of the native population, out of a total of 10,259 workers. To maintain a workforce unable to organize effectively against them, plantation managers decided to diversify their labor force, and in 1868 the first Japanese arrived to work on the plantations.

Like Chinese, Japanese migration had accelerated under integration, under the duress of Western military pressures. But unlike China, prior to the 1853 arrival of Commodore Matthew Perry and his four "black ships," Japanese had largely remained at home. The prior example of China's dismal fate, and Perry's irrefutable demands, led Japan to sign its first unequal treaty in 1854. It also embarked on the Meiji Restoration in 1868, a concerted and impressively effective national program to modernize and empower Japan by fortifying its military, revamping its economy, and strengthening its nation-state formations in emulation of the Western powers that by then dominated so much of the world, including the once-mighty China. Japan was so successful that within a few decades it would defeat its two larger neighbors in war: China in 1895, thereby gaining its first colony of Taiwan; and Russia in 1905.

Japan's impressive transformation was built upon the sacrifices of the peasant and small-farmer classes' heavy share of the tax burden. Displacement from their landholdings produced a mass of workers ready to leave, both to manage economic dislocation but also to avoid the 1873 Conscription Act, which motivated Japanese families to send away sons until they were past the age of military service. More than any other Asian state, the Japanese government managed the migration of its subjects with an eye toward bolstering its international standing by developing

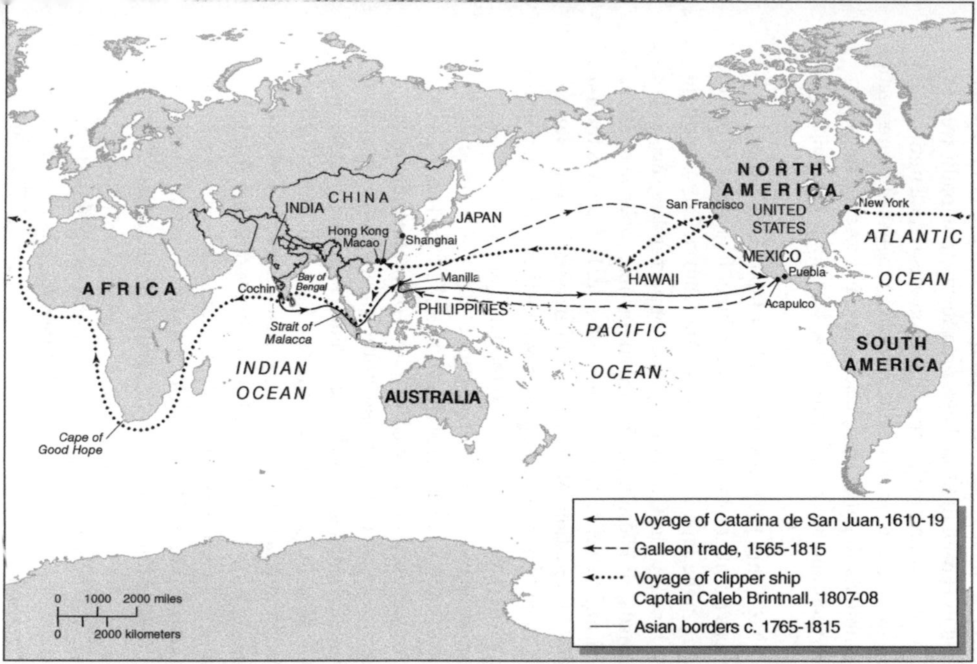
NORTH AMERICA
UNITED STATES
MEXICO
New York
San Francisco
Puebla
Acapulco
ATLANTIC OCEAN
SOUTH AMERICA
HAWAII
PACIFIC OCEAN
PHILIPPINES
Manilla
JAPAN
Shanghai
CHINA
INDIA
Hong Kong
Macao
Bay of Bengal
Cochin
Strait of Malacca
INDIAN OCEAN
AUSTRALIA
AFRICA
Cape of Good Hope
0 1000 2000 miles
0 2000 kilometers
Voyage of Catarina de San Juan,1610-19
Galleon trade, 1565-1815
Voyage of clipper ship Captain Caleb Brintnall, 1807-08
Asian borders c. 1765-1815

2. Through the voyage of Caterina de San Juan (1610–1619), the journey of clipper ship captain Caleb Brintnall (1807–1808), and routes of the galleon trade (1565–1815), this map traces travels linking Asia and the Americas over four centuries.

colonies abroad, supervising reactions to the presence of Japanese overseas, and imposing restrictions on emigration as deemed necessary. Under these conditions, the first group of 149 Japanese arrived in Hawaii in 1869; however, they were so badly treated during plantation life that the migration was halted until 1885. Once acceptable terms had been worked out between the respective governments, Japanese migration resumed under official supervision, and became a highly attractive option in certain regions.

From 1868 until 1941, over one million Japanese ventured overseas as emigrants and colonizers, including about 270,000 settling in the Japanese colonies of Manchuria, Taiwan, and the Korean peninsula. Others sought out opportunities such as fishing in Canada, rice farming in Northern Borneo, coffee plantations in Brazil, and nickel mining in New Caldonia. Hawaii was the most popular destination. At least 231,206 arrived between 1868 and 1929, including many peasants drawn by the belief that they could "earn 400 yen in three years" to return home "clad in brocade." Japanese increased from 0.1 percent of the workforce in 1882 (15 workers) to 73.4 percent in 1902 (31,029 workers) (Takaki 1998, 298). As they had with Chinese, plantation managers feared overreliance on any one ethnic group of workers and as anticipated, Japanese workers convened significant strikes in 1900, 1906, and 1909. As a result, the Hawaiian Sugar Planters Association scrambled to diversify their workforce. Chinese were no longer an option after the United States officially claimed control of Hawaii and applied its immigration restrictions, and so Portuguese, Puerto Ricans, African Americans from Tennessee, Koreans, and Filipinos joined Hawaii's complicated ethnic mix.

Korea was the next to experience the upheavals of forced integration into international economic and political systems, also producing migrations to the Americas. The so-called "Hermit Kingdom" had fended off both US and French warships since 1866, but finally succumbed to the military aggressions of neighboring Japan and signed the Treaty of Kanghwa in 1876. Other international powers

16

followed suit and the United States secured commensurate advantageous rights and trade terms in 1882. As their economy and sovereignty declined precipitously, Koreans struggled over questions of national culture and their future. In this factionalized setting, Japan steadily increased its influence, gradually removing Korea from China's traditional sphere of influence, and culminating in the outright annexation of Korea as a colony in 1910. Koreans coped in part by turning to Christianity (in their case missionaries were not associated with imperialist invasion) and other religions and covert political resistance, particularly in the case of the tens of thousands who departed overland to Chinese and Russian territories. In the meantime, the American missionary doctor Horace Allen became a trusted advisor to the royal family, and his ties to the Hawaiian Sugar Planters Association brokered the recruitment of about seven thousand Korean plantation workers between 1902 and 1905. Another one thousand went to Mexico but were badly treated, leading the Korean government to end the outflow, as it did in the case of Hawaii in 1905, and after 1910, Korea became wholly subject to Japanese-imposed restrictions. In 1906, Hawaii witnessed its first recruitment of Filipinos.

Despite the Philippines' long history of colonization and consequent overseas mobility, Filipinos were the last major Asian group who migrated to Hawaii. They had become subjects of the United States in 1898, an unanticipated and unwanted outcome of the Spanish American War fought over Cuban independence. After long agitations of their own, Filipinos took the opportunity to press for their independence as well, only to have Spain hand sovereignty over to the United States. Years of savage repression and resistance followed—a deadly imposition of US rule that still reverberated as the first trickle of Filipinos arrived in 1906. Filipinos developed their own version of "Hawaii fever" in the coming decades, however, with the growing institutionalization of American control, their unrestricted mobility as "nationals" traveling within the bounds of the US empire, and steadily declining economic conditions at home. Between 1907 and 1935,

122,100 traveled to Hawaii, with numbers increasing in the late 1920s after the 1924 Immigration Act banned the entry of all other Asians. Living and working together on plantations, Hawaii's diverse labor population developed a common language known as pidgin, reflective of a communal culture and priorities, so that even though Filipinos comprised 29.4 percent of the workforce in 1920, they joined with Japanese as the two largest groups in a multiethnic coalition that implemented a five-month strike which successfully produced pay raises and more benefits. Thirty-six percent eventually returned to the Philippines, while about 50,000 migrated to the mainland in the 1920s and 1930s.

Land of Eastern opportunities

The thickening tendrils of global interconnections that brought successive waves of different Asian nationalities to Hawaii foretold and paralleled the timing and patterns of migrations to the United States, although the available economic opportunities were much more diverse even as tensions over racial differences and inequalities sharply curtailed social, cultural, and political integration. The questions instigated by Asian immigration—including that of what racial groups could claim constitutional ideals for equality and US citizenship—would produce the United States' first attempts to systematically control its borders and limit the rights of immigrants and visitors.

Before these restrictions arose, merchants and students pioneered Chinese quests for American opportunities. A handful of students joined Hopu and 'Opukaha'ia at the Cornwall school during the 1820s with missionary sponsorship. In 1847, several merchants fled declining conditions in Guangzhou to test the waters in San Francisco; they were among the earliest to receive word of the discovery of gold at Sutter's Mill, news which they transmitted back to Hong Kong and fellow Cantonese. Credit ticket systems enabled tens of thousands of Chinese, peaking at twenty thousand in 1852, to leave behind crop failures and limited work options and embark for what is still known as the Gold Mountain. Most Chinese did not find gold on the streets, but enough newly rich men returned home to firmly establish the dream of fortunes to be had through hard work and determination in America.

Chinese began settling on the West Coast just as it was developing economically under American propulsion. The more languid ranching and small-scale fishing and farming that had prevailed under Spanish then Mexican rule was rapidly displaced. Yankee Americans pushed commercial agriculture, mining, manufacturing, and trading, abetted by Chinese and many other newly arrived immigrants such as Irish, Italians, and Chileans, who arrived at the West Coast seeking their fortunes.

Gold constituted only the most glamorous form of riches to be found in California. Thwarted by the vicissitudes of luck and hostility from other miners, Chinese drew upon their many experiences of migration and adversity and readily turned to the copious other opportunities available: silver and gold mines elsewhere in the west such as Nevada, Idaho, and Montana; fishing; manufacturing of goods such as cigars, textiles, boots, shoes, and brooms; import-export businesses; labor recruiting; service niches such as restaurants, laundries, and domestic service; large-scale manual labor projects such as railroad construction; farming at all levels from hired work crews performing backbreaking labor such as land reclamation, ditch digging, and stoop farming; independent small-scale farming; and managing and owning commercial farms. The peak of employment of Chinese labor was perhaps the 12,000—or 90 percent of the workforce—who constructed the western half of the Transcontinental Railroad.

Chinese made their way into many arenas of American life. Between 1872 and 1882, about 120 lived with families in New England, studying at local schools and colleges and preparing to become Chinese officials in the first systematically organized study abroad program, called the Chinese Educational Mission. From ports in southern China and particularly Hong Kong, Chinese merchants developed trans-Pacific trade, sending from China tea, sugar, chinaware, prepared opium, preserved foods, and Chinese medicines, while counterparts in San Francisco exported Californian abalone, metal, wheat flour, ginseng, gold, silver, timber, and remittances. They also provided credit to other Chinese and managed the labor recruiting system. San Francisco newspapers reported the first Chinese restaurant in 1849 and the photographer Ka Chau opened a portrait studio in 1854. As California and other parts of the American West developed, Chinese and later Japanese, Filipinos, and to a lesser degree Koreans and Punjabis filled enormous needs for labor building roads, mining, lumberyards, fisheries, and were intrinsic to the economic development of the western United States.

Although barely acknowledged in standard American histories, Asians came to America via pathways that were becoming increasingly well-established. For example, the herbal doctor Ing Hay and his merchant partner Lung On became well-respected pillars of the small town of John Day in eastern Oregon by following such routes. By the 1860s, gold could be found in many western districts, pulling fortune seekers beyond California and east of the Cascade Mountains. A Chinese merchant established the Kam Wah Chung Company, which he sold to Ing Hay and Lung On in 1887. Lung On had settled in John Day after staying briefly in San Francisco. He was well-educated in Chinese and English and an experienced businessman. Assessing the possibilities, he decided to establish himself in eastern Oregon, where he first met Ing Hay, who had arrived in the area in 1885 directly from China in the company of his father and following the advice of uncles living in Walla Walla, Washington. The two men combined their skills and remained in business together for more than fifty years, serving both Chinese and non-Chinese customers by running a general-goods store that also sold Chinese imports and served as a labor recruitment center, postal service, and herbal medical diagnostic service and pharmacy.

Japanese began systematically joining Chinese in the quest for American opportunities during the 1880s. The first wave consisted mostly of a handful of students seeking skills and knowledge associated with modernity, a quest produced by the many recent upheavals. In 1871, Japan's first ambassador to the United States, Mori Arinori, brought a few male and female students to study on the East Coast in aid of the Meiji enlightenment effort. Far more Japanese had to rely upon themselves. For example, Abiko Kyutaro left his family, who had a small business, to study English in Tokyo, intending eventually to move to the United States. He converted to Christianity in 1883 and sailed from Yokohama in 1885, arriving in San Francisco with only $1 in hand. Like many other so-called "schoolboys," he worked while attending school in hopes of gaining a better future. Abiko worked as a "houseboy" in a private home while attending grammar school. After graduation, he attended the University of California at Berkeley. During the 1890s, college-educated Asians did not gain professional employment and Abiko started a laundry business, acted as a labor recruiter, and then added a restaurant to his professional interests, but he made only modest profits. Abiko's real fortune came from running the Japanese-language newspaper *Nichibei Shimbun*, and financing and recruiting Japanese Americans to cooperative farms.

The Japanese government managed the first decade of Japanese migrations to Hawaii, the United States, and elsewhere in the Americas, but by the mid-1890s it had handed control over to emigration companies that operated according to its detailed restrictions. Laboring-class Japanese began arriving in droves; between 1885 through World War I, about three hundred thousand Japanese went to the United States, where they followed Chinese into agriculture, lumber camps, fisheries, and small businesses such as hostels and restaurants. Earlier arrivals,

English-speakers, and those able to accumulate capital could establish themselves as brokers both serving and profiting from their own communities.

Ushijima Kinji emigrated early, in 1889, determined to learn English as a schoolboy. He immediately changed his name to George Shima. Like Abiko, he worked his way up from domestic service, becoming a migrant farm laborer in the Sacramento Delta, but he soon turned to labor recruiting, supplying Japanese farm workers to white farmers. By the late 1890s, he had grown prosperous enough to lease land and begin his own farming operations. He expanded his operations into the San Joaquin Delta, where he experimented with soil types and potatoes, becoming dominant enough in potato production to gain the title of "Potato King" of California, by controlling 28,000 acres in production in 1913.

Asians who migrated to the West Coast later did not manage to ascend economically to become independent farmers or establish businesses. For example, about 7,300 Koreans entered in the brief window between 1903 and 1910 to follow Chinese and Japanese into the fields of California, but they remained primarily working-class; they were joined by about fifty thousand Filipinos, with the first large group arriving in 1923. As in Hawaii, Filipinos remained clustered at the bottom rungs socioeconomically: about 80 percent were migratory laborers, with earlier arrivals occupying the better available options of small businesses, farm management, or leasing land. Indians were another later arriving group, in 1904, as Punjabi workers began arriving in the Pacific Northwest with the guidance of labor recruiters and railroad agents, by following the tracks of the British Empire beyond the Commonwealth holdings of Hong Kong to arrive on the North American continent through Vancouver. Identifying higher wages and openings in lumber camps and fisheries, they crossed south to the United States in search of work.

Smaller numbers of Asians followed older routes to arrive through the East Coast. New York's Chinatown dates to the 1860s. During the 1880s, traders from Hooghly in West Bengal made their way to Southampton, England, and then crossed the Atlantic by steamer to New York, from whence they would disperse to peddle their wares by following the pathways of US leisure travelers and consumers—to the beach boardwalks of New Jersey, southern cities such as New Orleans, and tourist destinations in the Caribbean and Central America. During World War I, Indian maritime workers, toiling in the engine rooms and kitchens of British steamships they had signed onto in Calcutta and Bombay, jumped ship at New York, Philadelphia, and Baltimore, seeking better pay and less brutal and slave-like work conditions. Upon landing, they followed networks inland as far as Detroit, finding employment in steel, shipbuilding, and munitions industries, while in New York City they entered the service economy as line cooks, dishwashers, doormen, and elevator operators in Manhattan hotels and restaurants.

Like the vast majority of immigrants who came to the US between 1850 and 1930 (that is, the roughly thirty-five million Europeans), most of the almost one million Chinese, Japanese, Koreans, Filipinos, and Indians who arrived were also seeking to better their fortunes and improve their lives. Their dispersion across so much of the United States, and their ready participation in many areas of the developing American economy, reflects the capacity for the young republic to absorb the aspiration and energies of literally millions from all corners of the earth. Unlike their European peers, however, the incorporation of Asians into the US nation-state required a century of struggle and negotiation regarding qualifications for citizenship and the legal categories and racial attributions conferring such rights.

American ambivalence

Despite their apparent usefulness to American economic development, particularly in its western states and territories, the United States was deeply anxious and ambivalent about Asian immigration, particularly that of laborers. Asians arrived in significant numbers during an era when racial differences and inequalities were believed to be a matter of the latest science, with Darwin's *Origin of Species* (1859) seeming to authorize beliefs not only in evolution, but also in competition between species, survival of the fittest, and thus extinction of the weak and triumph of the strong, thereby naturalizing conflict between nations and races, encouraging the "science" of eugenics, and requiring segregation. Asians had not only arrived from other geographic places and climates, which were presumed to nurture essentially discrete civilizations and biological traits, but also embodied the visual markers of their difference in their hair, skin color, facial features, and bone structure.

Could the boundaries of the American republic, founded by Europeans, prove sufficiently elastic to incorporate such different races? Asian immigration forced the United States to confront key questions concerning its racial borders around eligibility for citizenship and, for those groups deemed unfit, whether and how to limit entry and settlement. More so than any other group, Asians, who were racialized as a "Yellow Peril" invasion, challenged the United States' constitutional claims of equality for all with the problem of whether racially distinct, trans-Pacific arrivals could participate on equal terms in the "nation of immigrants" with those from Europe. If not, should groups found incapable of becoming American be allowed to immigrate at all? And, what sovereign powers did the nation-state hold to enact such restrictions against the citizens of other states?

Chapter 2
Race and the American republic

Perhaps the most famous Asian Americans immigrated early in the history of the US republic. The so-called "Siamese Twins," Chang and Eng Bunker, arrived in 1829 at the age of seventeen, brought by Captain Abel Coffin to Boston from Thailand. The pair were of Chinese and Malaysian heritage and conjoined by a ligature of skin at their chests. Nonetheless, from a young age they had helped support their family by fishing, peddling goods, and raising and selling duck eggs. Upon meeting Coffin, they signed a contract to accompany him, but they had not originally intended to leave permanently.

Over the course of the next few years, Coffin exhibited the young men to great profit through every state of the union and much of Europe, Panama, Cuba, and southern Canada. As soon as Chang and Eng reached full legal adulthood, they sued for independence and took control of their destinies by adopting the surname of good friends, becoming US citizens, managing their own appearances, and using the considerable proceeds to establish themselves in highly respectable American lives. They became prosperous farmers, owning land and slaves in North Carolina, and married two sisters, Sallie and Adelaide Yates, with whom they fathered more than ten children each. The occasional tours that supplemented their farming incomes showcased their physical strength and their high levels of acculturation, and disseminated knowledge of their homeland. The twins died within hours of each other in 1874, having not only traversed vast distances and cultural and racial divides, but also having attained considerable economic and social success while claiming new lives in the United States.

Despite—or, indeed, perhaps because of—their racial and biological singularity, the Bunker twins were able to become Americans in ways that would be almost entirely denied to other Asians during the era of Asian exclusion that extended from 1882 until 1952. Asian immigration tested American ideals of equality with the problem of whether all racial groups could be integrated into American democracy. The experiences of the Bunker twins notwithstanding, by law Asian immigrants were banned from citizenship by naturalization for most of US history, dating back to the 1790 Nationality Act, which restricted this right to "free white persons," which in practice meant property-owning white men, which lasted until 1952. That the Bunker twins gained such status reflects the uneven application of laws and the many different considerations at play in shaping attitudes and institutional practices regarding whether and how Asians could claim rights and belonging in the United States.

The Bunkers benefited from the timing and location of their arrival and settlement, as well as their youth and adaptability in conjunction with their physical anomaly. Asians were too few in number on the East Coast during the mid-nineteenth century to be considered much more than exotic oddities, and thus unthreatening to the existing racial order. Their celebrity and demonstrated attainments also fended off hostility, as did the elite status and advantages associated with the few dozen Asians who came as students or for business purposes in programs such as the Chinese Educational Mission (1872–1882), the sponsorship of students by Japanese diplomat Mori Arinori, or the circulation of Bengali traders. In contrast, proximity made the West Coast, and particularly California, the chief destination for Asian migrants in areas with lower populations and less institutionalized control by the federal government. These uncertain conditions fostered tremendous anxieties about competing cultures and the maintenance of US control in this contact zone between eastward and westward migrations. Outright hostilities rapidly boiled over, fueled by racial antagonisms, economic competition, and the need to clarify the sovereign powers of the young nation of the United States over matters of border control.

At its starkest, the dangerous "Yellow Peril" was framed as a contest between free and unfree labor, marked by ascribed racial differences in which white men had the free will and independent thinking to exercise citizenship in the American republic, whereas Asians, particularly on the West Coast, bore the stigma of unfree coolie labor. Credit systems controlled by labor recruiters and other brokers fueled the image of Asian workers as producing new forms of slavery, at a time when the young republic had barely survived the bitter Civil War concerning this form of labor. Chinese migrants borrowed money for the cost of passage, to be repaid through a set number of years of labor at fixed wages secured by contracts. These practices fueled the image of Chinese as "unfree" coolie workers, requiring rejection in law. In the thick of the Civil War, a Republican-controlled Congress sought to forestall Southern planters' plans to replace African slaves with Chinese coolies by passing "An act to prohibit the 'coolie trade' by American citizens in American vessels" in 1862. The law was never enforced because its definition of "coolie" was too vague, but it nevertheless portended future legislation that linked the perception of unfree coolie Asian workers to African slavery.

In contrast, just a few years later, in the thick of constructing the Transcontinental Railroad, the United States sought to guarantee its access to Chinese workers by signing the 1868 Burlingame Treaty with the Chinese government, guaranteeing reciprocal rights of free migration and emigration. The completion of that great national-industrial project the very next year shortened travel times from coast to coast to only three weeks, securing the territorial integrity of the United States, consolidating the economy across the continent, but also rendering "Yellow Peril"

3. The political cartoonist Thomas Nast paired the themes of "The nigger must go" and "The Chinese must go" to satirize the racial limits of American democracy. Nast's commentary on the anti-Chinese movement appeared on the cover of *Harper's Weekly*, September 13, 1879.

invasion a plausible threat for the entire country. If American Yankees could more readily migrate westward riding the railroad, so too could the uncountable hordes of Chinese swarming the West Coast travel further east.

A complex array of competing interests and priorities shaped US decisions regarding the restricting of Asian immigration and citizenship rights, which laid the foundations for ideological and institutional strategies delimiting general practices of admission and inclusion into the American republic. Immigration policy and law are so fiercely contested because they affect the core interests of many competing constituencies: white labor organizations combatting competition pitted against large- and small-scale businesses seeking cheaper, more controllable workers; trade groups, missionaries, and internationalists hoping to promote US influence overseas decrying nativists defending the nation's racial purity; while liberals citing constitutional ideals of equality worked with marginalized ethnic and religious communities in seeking more egalitarian access.

The United States' first attempts to enact border controls drew upon widespread beliefs in the scientific basis of eugenics to target Asians based on the attribution of their essential, biologically determined racial difference and inferiority. Their home governments were generally too weak or disinterested to protest effectively as the United States expanded its sovereign powers in limiting their mobility and settlement rights. Only the emerging world power of Japan—not the declining Chinese empire nor the colonized territories of Korea, the Philippines, or India—was in a position to joust with the United States regarding principles and enactments of immigration controls, a fight largely won by the United States in asserting its sovereign prerogatives as a nation-state to control its territory and the peoples seeking admission.

Asian immigration has been the chief forum through which the United States has worked out contradictions between its constitutional assertions of equal rights and the allocation of unequal status based on restricted legal rights of immigration and citizenship by naturalization. For most of US history, powerful beliefs in racial differences upheld the concept that only white men—preferably Protestant Christians of non-indentured status— possessed the individual capacities necessary to participate as citizens in a democratic nation. The 1790 Nationality Act limited the right of citizenship by naturalization to "free white persons," a restriction that institutionalized beliefs in the irreconcilable differences and natural hierarchies stemming from race and biological ancestry. Those eligible expanded over time, with Mexicans gaining citizenship rights when the United States annexed California and other western territories through the 1848 Treaty of Guadalupe Hidalgo, and African Americans gaining protections for their citizenship rights with the Thirteenth (1865) and Fourteenth Amendments (1868)— although citizenship did not secure full equality for these populations.

Asians, on the other hand, were a wholly immigrant, rather than already present, minority population. Assumptions that Asians were unassimilable and unable to wield the responsibilities of citizenship justified severe restrictions on their entry. For those already resident, segregationist beliefs compelled efforts to confine Asians physically, socially, and economically through restrictions on property ownership, lack of access to legal protections and public services, bans on interracial marriages, and employment limitations. These types of Asian exclusion were aspects of broader and deeply troubled efforts to restore and maintain the demography and culture of the thirteen original colonies. Through World War II, the problem posed by Asian immigration led the United States to draw on beliefs in racial difference to enact increasingly expansive, discriminatory immigration controls, which in turn extended its powers as a sovereign nation.

California: Epicenter of anti-Asian discrimination

As early as 1852, California governor John Bigler declared his intention to limit the entry of Chinese. Well into the twentieth century, Asian immigrants to the United States overwhelmingly settled in California; the state would pass several laws attempting to restrict their entry, by imposing taxes on shipowners transporting them and explicitly prohibiting the entry of "Mongolians" (the legal and racial term used for Asians generally at the time) and those ineligible for citizenship, only to have each effort cast aside as unconstitutional by courts which ruled that immigration was a matter of foreign commerce subject to regulation only by the federal government. California would have to wait three decades before its local "Yellow Peril" crisis gained sufficient national attention to become US law.

Alongside efforts to restrict immigration, local laws and statutes targeted and harassed Chinese, expressing institutionally the presumption that they had lesser claims to equal rights and protections in the United States. The statewide Foreign Miners Tax (1850, 1852) operated on this principle by extracting monthly fees; it was enforced primarily against Chinese by private contractors, sometimes by force and deceit. Chinese were highly vulnerable to violence in the frontier West, and had little recourse to the limited government protections available. The 1854 court ruling in *People v. Hall* categorized Chinese with African and Native Americans to prohibit them from testifying against whites in court. Consequently, few murderers of Chinese received punishment; the California state legislature reported in 1862 that eighty-eight Chinese were known to have been murdered by white people, eleven of whom were official Collectors of Foreign Miner's Tax, but in only two cases were the murderers convicted and hanged.

San Francisco was the epicenter of anti-Asian activism through World War II and passed local statutes that targeted specifically Chinese practices, illustrating how legal discriminations could be enacted without racial specifications. For example, the so-called Queue Ordinance of 1873 mandated that individuals held in county jail would have their hair cut unless they paid a fine. Supposedly a "sanitary" measure, this law unduly punished

Chinese who required their queues, or pigtails, in order to return to China.

Despite perceptions that they were incapable of adapting to life in the United States, Chinese and other Asians frequently turned to both the US court system and international laws to challenge discriminatory legislation by employing lawyers and lobbying various levels of government officials. The Fourteenth Amendment proved particularly critical to securing protections. Passed in 1868 to ensure the egalitarian integration of newly liberated African Americans, the law's wording guaranteed "equal protection" for those resident in the United States and birthright citizenship, regardless of race. Chinese court challenges established the legal precedents that the Fourteenth Amendment and its protections applied to *anyone* resident in the United States, as in the case of *Ho Ah Kow v. Nunan* (1879), which abolished the Queue Ordinance and other discriminatory laws. Despite their success in domestic court cases, however, Chinese would steadily lose ground in challenging immigration legislation governing their entry rights and citizenship, laying legal precedents for the exclusion of later waves of Asian migrants, and shrinking rights for immigrants overall.

Closing America's gates

The core of the unequal status of Asian immigrants stemmed from their ineligibility for citizenship by naturalization, a legal barrier that institutionalized the belief in their essential biological difference and inferiority, as first legislated with the 1790 Nationality Act. Asians battled consistently and unsuccessfully to challenge this racial categorization. Porous enforcement allowed the Bunker twins to naturalize, as did Yung Wing when he became the first Chinese to attain an American BA degree in 1854 from Yale University. By the 1870s, however, West Coast Chinese were widely viewed as an invasion of unfree coolie labor, associated with vice industries such as gambling, opium dens, and prostitution, the eating of taboo foods such as rats and dogs, and all manner of heathen practices. Chinese citizenship applications were routinely denied, with the 1878 California circuit court case *In re Ah Yup* establishing that despite the vagueness of the term "white persons," which could include individuals ranging from blue-eyed blonds to swarthy brunettes darker than Chinese, it "had a well-settled meaning in common popular speech and scientific literature" that did not include so-called Mongolians. If Chinese and other Asians could never hope to become US citizens, should they be allowed to continue immigrating at all?

Throughout the 1870s, pressures for immigration restriction gained national urgency as California's Chinese problem became a platform for both the Democratic and Republican parties. In a closely contested political climate, California held decisive votes in the Electoral College, which transformed its local Chinese problem into a crisis resounding across the continent. Severe economic contractions and widespread labor strikes and violence further inflamed anti-immigrant hostilities, even as the completion of the Transcontinental Railroad in 1869 made more plausible the possibility that California's "Mongolian hordes" could readily reach the East Coast. Targeting Chinese, who could not vote and were resident in tiny numbers, (only 0.2 percent of the national population in 1880), the United States resolved to change course and begin closing its doors to select groups of immigrants categorized by race and class. Through the narrowing of its gates to Chinese, the US government developed rationales that would later justify the selective closing of its borders more generally, along with mechanisms for immigration control that could operate legally and bureaucratically within the framework of international law and relationships.

As early as 1874, President Ulysses S. Grant had expressed his willingness to support legal restrictions on Chinese immigration, if a suitable means could be found to do so. The next year, Congress passed the Page Act, restricting the general importation of criminals and prostitutes. In practice, the law was enforced primarily against Chinese women, who were presumed to be prostitutes. The numbers of Chinese women entering through San Francisco fell dramatically, setting a precedent for severely diminishing entry rights for Chinese and contributing to a gender imbalance in Chinese immigration that persisted into the 1970s.

More extensive exclusion of Chinese foundered against presidential fears that such racially explicit immigration bars would offend the Chinese government, thereby harming trade and other international connections, such as diplomatic and missionary projects, and undermining the extraterritorial status of US citizens in China. The 1879 "Fifteen Passenger Bill," which limited the number of Chinese passengers per ship, drew the ire of the Chinese minister stationed in Washington, DC, who found it insulting and pointed out that it violated the 1868 Burlingame Treaty's terms securing free migration for both Chinese and Americans. President Rutherford B. Hayes acknowledged that the bill attempted to almost completely ban Chinese immigration, "an unprecedented attempt by the legislative branch to nullify a treaty with a friendly foreign power," and vetoed the bill. Hayes indicated his willingness to impose restrictions, but required renegotiation of the Burlingame Treaty, to develop terms acceptable to the Chinese government.

Congress and the White House acted swiftly to advance the Angell Treaty of 1880, which gained Chinese acknowledgment of the United States' sovereign right to "regulate, limit, or suspend" the coming or residence of Chinese laborers. Those categorized as "teachers, students, merchants, or from curiosity, together with their body and household servants, and Chinese laborers who are now in the United States" retained entry rights and "all the rights, privileges, immunities, and exemptions which are accorded to the citizens and subjects of the most favored nation." After some tinkering with how long the law should remain in effect (again with presidential warnings to avoid offending the Chinese government), in 1882 Congress passed what was initially known as the Chinese Restriction Act, under the title "An Act to execute certain treaty stipulations relating to Chinese" and received, at last, the signature of President Chester A. Arthur.

Despite the negotiated terms for Chinese restriction, American implementation of the law proved much more severe than Chinese officials had expected in permitting entry only to those of the explicitly stated exempt classes. The law also did not fulfill American expectations that it would end Chinese immigration altogether, and major outbursts of anti-Chinese violence broke out—in 1885 in Rock Springs, Wyoming, then in the Tacoma and Seattle areas later the same year, in efforts to expel Chinese who remained physically resident and working, despite the bars against their entry. The federal government began to develop the enforcement personnel and bureaucratic capacities needed to enforce the laws, which required policing of the United States' long land borders to both the north and south, strategies to evaluate which Chinese could legitimately claim entry as one of the "6 exempt classes," and measures to identify, discourage, and punish the new crimes of unlawful entry and residency produced by the restrictions. The construction of such defensive walls led Chinese to develop sophisticated and largely effective strategies for continued migration; in response, the immigration bureaucracy implemented a thickening tangle of laws and bureaucratic obstacles such as status verification, evidence and documentation, interrogation, confinement, and the persistent threats of discovery and deportation.

Chinese noncompliance produced refinements and extensions of the original law. The 1888 Scott Act eliminated one exempt category as subject to excessive fraud, and the 1892 Geary Act extended the laws for another decade, while requiring that all resident Chinese register and that every Chinese immigrant, defined by race, carry a Certificate of Residence to verify his or her legal entry. Only Chinese were required to apply for and carry this precursor to the green card, which bore similarities to documentation required of free blacks before Emancipation. The Geary Act also authorized the use of deportation for illegal immigrants, which became a looming shadow in the lives of exclusion-era Chinese. Under the leadership of the Chinese Consolidated Benevolent Association (an umbrella organization commonly known as the Six Companies), following the advice of legal counsel Chinese challenged this new discrimination by filing the Fong Yueting (149 U.S. 698 (1893)) test case in court. To their shock and dismay, they lost, as the Supreme Court affirmed the United States' sovereign and plenary powers over immigration. With this ruling, all racially Chinese people physically within the United States were presumed to be present illegally and deportable until they could produce their certificate documenting legal entry as long as the Chinese exclusion laws remained in effect.

The US government's assertiveness in claiming authority to control immigration was possible in part because the Chinese government had so little power to protest effectively. Its repeated efforts to renegotiate treaty terms to protect Chinese in the United States had no impact as the US government continued to expand its sovereign powers. Chinese exclusion set the basis for the United States' evolution into a border-keeping nation that established precedents and foundational principles as well for other countries that adopted parallel presumptions and practices of why, whom, and how to regulate admission into their territories. The lack of political power by Chinese in the United States or the Chinese government allowed the United States to turn away from free immigration to controlling its borders, claiming growing powers in its abiding, often frustrated, preoccupation with excluding particular categories of unwanted migrants by imposing new forms of inequalities based on immigration status with an expanding array of targets, and a growing bureaucracy for enforcement of laws that were subject to systematic evasion and outright fraud. The Angel Island Immigration Station, which operated from 1910 until closed by a fire in 1940 in the San Francisco Bay, emerged as the chief symbol of exclusion where migrants from all origins, but chiefly Chinese, were detained while immigration authorities evaluated their identity and status claims. Most immigrants remained only a few days at most, but the average Chinese stay was a couple of weeks, which could stretch into a couple of years while interrogations and disputes worked their way through the system.

In 1891, Congress passed a general immigration law barring entry to paupers, the diseased, and the illiterate, and authorizing establishment of a formally constituted Immigration Bureau to implement these restrictions. The US immigration agency gained an expanding array of powers to determine the legal admissibility of aspiring immigrants, who experienced a steady diminishment of their rights and claims for legal protections in the United States. Between 1897 and 1906, organized labor leaders controlled the Immigration Bureau and attempted complete exclusion of Chinese, turning away even legally exempt diplomats, merchants, and students on the slightest of pretexts, using humiliating procedures. As before, Chinese attempted to challenge their hostile decisions by appealing to the courts, which applied more reasonable standards of evidence. However, a series of judicial rulings cumulatively lodged decisive powers with the Immigration Bureau over immigration cases, eroding the rights of potential immigrants to protections such as lawyers and access to US courts. In the 1905 Ju Toy case (198 U.S. 253 (1905)), for example, the Supreme Court ruled that even Chinese claiming rights of entry as US citizens could not appeal to judicial processes.

The only major case won by Chinese was the 1898 Supreme Court case of Wong Kim Ark (169 U.S. 649 (1898)), which ruled that the Fourteenth Amendment's guarantee of birthright citizenship applied to anyone born in the United States, even to Asians who could not naturalize. To the dismay of immigration authorities, US-born Chinese and other Asian Americans held citizenship and could travel to and from the United States. This outcome provided a critical toehold for Asians to claim American lives, even as ineligibility for citizenship by naturalization provided a key strategy for attempting their exclusion. Until the repeal of Chinese exclusion in 1943, the main venue for legal entry by Chinese stemmed from arduously verified claims on birthright citizenship that also produced the main loopholes for fraudulent entry known as the paper-son, or slot, system.

Amid rising tides of American nativism, the Chinese government's efforts to negotiate better treatment for Chinese migrants provoked Congress to vote to impose immigration restrictions unilaterally and in perpetuity in 1904. In protest the following year, Chinese merchants and students led a boycott of American goods that extended from cities in China to Southeast Asia demanding that the entry rights of Chinese legally allowed to do so be upheld. This demonstration of Chinese nationalist anger led President Theodore Roosevelt to issue an executive order commanding the Immigration Bureau to treat exempt Chinese respectfully. Although these few permitted classes continued to enter under the stigma of being Chinese, their experiences improved thereafter. Nonetheless, to be Chinese and living in America, regardless of citizenship status, was to subsist in the margins.

Having secured Chinese exclusion, nativists quickly turned their energies to other groups of as-yet-unrestricted migrants from Asia. The few hundreds of Indians who had started crossing into Washington State from Vancouver in 1904 faced violence within a few years. Several hundred members of the Asiatic Exclusion League attacked and sought to expel local lumberyard workers, who were predominantly Sikhs, in 1907. The men were rounded up, beaten, and more than a hundred removed to British Columbia. Others fled elsewhere across the West Coast, only to run into similar hostilities.

Despite the visibility of the "tide of turbans," Japanese presented a greater menace. With the anti-Chinese laws in place, Japanese became the largest Asian community in the United States, increasing from 85,716 in 1900 to 152,745 in 1910, while the numbers of Chinese fell over the same years from 118,746 to 94,414. Japanese had replaced Chinese in the fields and clustered in many of the same occupational and small-business niches. In contrast to Chinese, however, Japanese in America endured the protection and scrutiny of their homeland, which was a rising world power highly sensitive to slights against its national reputation. The Japanese government actively sought to avoid the negative stereotypes and treatment allocated to Chinese by encouraging Japanese Americans to dress neatly, maintain personal hygiene, form families, emphasize their hardworking and law-abiding traits, and avoid the vice industries associated with Chinese. It also acted expediently to protect the national standing of Japan, even if this required measures detrimental to the living conditions of Japanese Americans.

California's Anti-Asiatic League launched their attacks against Japanese by protesting their attendance in integrated schools in San Francisco. In the face of such local upheavals, President Theodore Roosevelt sought to avoid an international conflict by brokering the Gentlemen's Agreement with the Japanese government in 1907. In contrast to the nearly unilateral, and humiliating, imposition of US controls against Chinese, the Japanese government assumed responsibility for enacting restrictions on its own subjects by withholding passports from laborers. In return, it gained the face-saving measures of continued attendance in integrated schools, rather than segregation into the "Oriental" schools which Chinese attended, and for legal migration by elites such as merchants, students, diplomats, tourists, and the parents, wives, and children of bona fide US residents. The Japanese American community continued to grow despite the Gentlemen's Agreement, because women arrived as "picture brides" and produced families. The prohibition against laborers, however, eradicated Japanese American labor-recruiting businesses. Korean migration ended as well when Japan formally annexed the peninsula as a colony in 1910.

The Gentlemen's Agreement saved face for the Japanese government while advancing the United States' anti-Asian exclusionary agendas. The two governments' ability to negotiate such terms reflected the emerging international consensus regarding the powers of sovereign nations to control their borders. In principle, the Japanese government accepted the US government's authority to restrict immigration, but it preferred that controls be enacted with respect for a nation of equal standing.

Exclusion and empire

The expansion of exclusion contradicted the United States' unfurling embrace of its Pacific destiny. America's colonization of the Philippines in 1898, along with Puerto Rico, and its outright annexation of Hawaii in 1898, extended its territorial reach across the Pacific but underscored its ambivalence about Asian subjects. Complementing the intent of the Chinese exclusion laws and the Gentlemen's Agreement, the federal government broke with past practice in not allocating Filipinos citizen status. In past territorial acquisitions, such as contiguous territory like Mexico, areas with inhabitants racialized as white like Puerto Rico, and Hawaii with its long history of US influence, the United States had granted citizenship to residents. Asian Filipinos, however, merely became "nationals" who gained rights of free migration within US territories, but not citizenship and the accompanying franchise. Further delimiting its racial boundaries, the United States also applied its immigration restrictions to these newly acquired territories so that Chinese and Japanese could not enter them and then seek to migrate to the United States.

Demonstrating beliefs in the decisive connections between racial difference and geography, the next major restrictions against Asian entry targeted regions of origin, revealing a further evolution in how discriminatory immigration laws could be framed without resorting to explicitly racial terms. In 1917, Congress enacted the Barred Zone Act, banning immigration for peoples from an area extending from Indonesia to Turkey. Along with this sweeping exclusion based on geography, the law designated a wider array of unwelcome types by traits: "imbeciles, epileptics, alcoholics, poor, criminals, beggars, any person suffering attacks of insanity...those who have any form of dangerous contagious disease, aliens who have a physical disability that will restrict them from earning a living in the United States...polygamists and anarchists," radicals, and anyone involved with prostitution. The 1917 Barred Zone Act also specified categories of welcome migrants who retained entry rights, including students along with "Government officers, ministers or religious teachers, missionaries, lawyers, physicians, chemists, civil engineers, teachers...authors, artists, merchants, and travelers for curiosity or pleasure...their legal wives or their children under sixteen years of age." The open discrimination girding this law led the Indian Nobel Prize winner in literature Rabindranath Tagore to cut short his 1929 visit with the explanation that even "Jesus could not get into America, because, first of all, He would not have the necessary money, and secondly, He would be an Asiatic." Through this law, the United States further clarified its conceptions of wanted and unwanted traits in individual immigrants, but for Asians, the defining criterion was race although select categories such as students, diplomats, and merchants, could arrive on a temporary basis.

Such segregation at the United States' borders paralleled laws that enacted forms of segregation domestically, occasionally revealing the irrationalities and inconsistencies in race-based demarcations. Apart from Japanese, Asian children largely attended segregated schools. In *Gong Lum v. Rice* (275 U.S. 78 (1927)), for example, the Supreme Court ruled that Martha Lum was "colored" and therefore had to attend the "colored" school in Rosedale, Mississippi. In response, the Lum family moved to Arkansas, where anti-Chinese segregation was more porous. In 1939, fourteen states had anti-miscegenation laws prohibiting marriages between Asians and whites. Despite such barriers, Filipino Salvador Roldan managed to marry a British woman, Marjorie Rogers, in Los

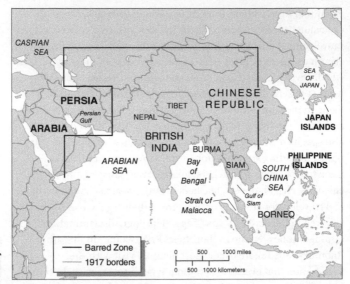

4. The 1917 Immigration Act stated that "persons who are natives of islands not possessed by the United States adjacent to the Continent of Asia" were banned completely from immigrating into the United States. The Barred Zone extended from Indonesia through the Southeast Asian peninsula, India, and western China to much of contemporary Iran, Turkmenistan, Uzbekistan, and the eastern tip of Saudi Arabia.

Angeles in 1933 by arguing that he was not "Mongolian," the restricted group specified in California law, but rather "Malay," which was not named in the law. His triumph was brief, for the California state legislature swiftly passed a new law including "Malays" and retroactively disallowing prior marriages with whites.

Asians faced many barriers in employment as well. Unions and professional organizations refused them membership and they could not get government jobs. For example, Frank Coloma passed the civil service examinations in both Washington and California but was refused employment in Seattle, Tacoma, and Los Angeles.

Despite his credentials, Coloma ended up working as a handyman/janitor in an apartment complex, choosing severe underemployment in the United States because conditions in the Philippines remained comparatively dire. The even more sweeping "alien land laws" sharply limited Asian immigrants' capability to own and lease property, based on their ineligibility for citizenship.

Japanese Americans went the furthest in challenging the legal ascription of racial inferiority to Asians. The shock of the Gentlemen's Agreement led them to shift course, under counsel from the Japanese government, in order to demonstrate that Japanese could display good citizenship and high levels of civilizational attainments. The Japanese Association of America (JAA) formed to coordinate efforts while both Japanese American leaders such as Abiko Kyutaro and George Shima and Japanese diplomatic personnel urged *issei*, or first-generation Japanese immigrants, to bring "picture brides," form respectable family units, and engage in agriculture, then thought to be a less threatening economic activity. *Issei* were urged to adopt behaviors associated with the American mainstream such as Western-style clothing, observance of the Sabbath and traditional American holidays, and avoidance of vice activities associated with Chinese such as prostitution, gambling, and opium. The aim was to demonstrate that Japanese were fully equal to white Americans, without seeking to erase that they were of an Asian race. The aspirational Japanese American leadership negotiated between the demands of the Japanese government that they uphold national honor by displaying respectability despite their increasingly restricted options for success, particularly in the western United States, and the strains of obscuring the less laudatory activities of their poorer, itinerant, working-class co-ethnics.

JAA head Shima set the pace in becoming the first Japanese American millionaire—by 1920, "The Potato King" produced about 85 percent of California's potato crop. For his part, Abiko sponsored cooperative farms in California's central valley and recruited Japanese American families to establish landholdings. Japanese made significant inroads at all levels of commercial agriculture, particularly in California and Washington, from the growing to the marketing of crops such as flowers, strawberries, asparagus, and grapes. The most successful of Japanese Americans, such as Shima and Abiko used their wealth and high levels of acculturation to claim the United States for Japanese, even as greater numbers confined to laboring classes continued to struggle with their diminishing circumstances.

Nonetheless, these demonstrations of economic attainment and adherence with mainstream American values only incensed exclusionary attacks. Not satisfied with the bar on laborers imposed with the Gentlemen's Agreement, Californians began agitating for further measures to uproot and dislocate Japanese. The 1913 Alien Land Law, versions of which would be adopted in Washington and seven other western states, banned "aliens ineligible for citizenship" from owning agricultural land. This legal category derived from the 1790 Nationality Act and targeted Asians, particularly Japanese, who had made the greatest inroads. The Japanese ambassador initially protested but then backed off, after deciding that naturalization was a "domestic" matter.

Such laws had limited impact at first, as *issei* placed land titles under the names of their second-generation, American-born children, the *Nisei*, or leased land, or placed land into shareholding companies. A revised law, passed by 70 percent of California voters in 1920, closed these loopholes so that ineligible aliens could not purchase or lease farmland, hold stocks in agricultural land-holding companies, transfer or sell agricultural land, and be guardians for minors holding title to such land. The 1920 law affected Japanese Americans much more severely than its 1913 precursor; the amount of Japanese-owned land decreased from 75,000 to 42,000 acres between 1920 and 1925, and leased lands from 192,150 to just over 76,000 acres. Washington State passed a similar law in 1921. After years of struggle to claim farms from marginal land and wilderness areas and establish stable lives, Japanese Americans faced confinement in the dead-end status of farm laborers, although some managed to use established relationships to non-Japanese to hold onto their farms.

A core issue in Japanese challenges to the Alien Land Laws was the question of their ineligibility for citizenship. Throughout the 1910s, they sought judicial clarification of the term "white" and whether it could include Japanese. These decisions were rendered through the major test case of *Ozawa v. U.S.* Born in Japan in 1875, Ozawa Takao had arrived in San Francisco in 1894 as a student. He worked while attending classes and studied at Berkeley before going to Honolulu in 1906, where he worked for a US company, married a Japanese American woman, and had two children. By the time he filed his case in 1914, Ozawa had attained a fully integrated life. He had lived in the United States for twenty-eight years and lacked ties to the Japanese consulate or Japanese American organizations. He spoke English all the time, his wife was American-educated, he had no Japanese friends, his children attended American schools and churches, and he presented evidence of his excellent character and work record. Could this "paragon" of the "assimilated Japanese immigrant" not gain citizenship solely because of his race?

Despite this immersion in American life, Ozawa lost repeatedly in court but kept appealing to higher courts, arguing that his cultural identity as American made him fit for citizenship. By the time he appealed to the Ninth Circuit Court in San Francisco in 1916, the mainland Japanese American community recognized his suitability as a test case. The Japanese Foreign Ministry, however, refused to take up the cause on the grounds that naturalization was a domestic issue for the US government. In return for this deference, when the case finally reached the highest level, the Supreme Court delayed taking action for several years to avoid offending the Japanese government at sensitive junctures. First World War I, and Japan's campaign for a racial equality clause in the Treaty of Versailles, and then military negotiations concerning naval arms, led it to put off announcing its decision until 1922, when it ruled conclusively that Ozawa was neither a free white person nor African by birth or descent and therefore could not naturalize because of his race. After so many years and setbacks, the Japanese American community was angered but not surprised. The Ozawa decision had undermined one of their key strategies for challenging the Alien Land Laws. In 1923, when the Supreme Court upheld the constitutionality of the Alien Land Laws as well, many Japanese Americans gave up on the United States altogether and pulled up stakes to seek brighter prospects in more hospitable places such as Brazil and Manchuria.

The racial bar against naturalization by Asians hardened the following year with the 1923 Supreme Court case of *Bhagat Singh Thind v. United States*. Thind had arrived as a student in 1913 but had fought in World War I and was still serving in the US military when he applied for naturalization in 1919. He followed in the footsteps of several dozen Indians who had already gained citizenship because racial categorization schemes considered Indians as Aryan or Caucasian, even though they were dark of skin and not Christian. In the case of Thind, however, the Supreme Court decided to break with past practices in setting aside the "scientific" findings of eugenics racial systems and instead based its judgment on the view of the "common man," which would never find Indians to be white. Thind lost his case and the Indians who had previously received citizenship lost this status retroactively. The Thind decision demonstrated the inconsistency and instability of racial categories, but nonetheless upheld them as constitutionally acceptable rationales for the allocation of unequal rights. Rounding out the barriers against Asians holding US citizenship, the 1922 Cable Act mandated that any American female citizen who married a man "ineligible for citizenship" assumed the status of her husband.

In 1924, Congress committed even more fully to the racial and geographic demarcation of the world by enacting into law the most sweeping and explicit expression of what races could be assimilated into the United States, and a system of immigration quotas that quantified the degree to which others were deemed more or less suitable racial stock. Isolationist and nativist public sentiments had been building with the surging immigration of the 1890s and 1900s, which included unprecedentedly high numbers of Jews and southern and eastern Europeans. The brutality and senselessness of World War I catalyzed a crisis of confidence regarding Western civilization that only intensified concerns about whether the United States could continue to absorb strains of so many different kinds of peoples, including radicals on the political left. In 1907, Congress appointed the Dillingham Commission, comprised primarily of advocates for restriction, to make a "scientific" study of eugenics, immigration patterns, and census data. Its findings, issued in 1911, framed the next half-century of immigration restrictions. The Dillingham Report urged that national cohesion receive primary consideration in immigration controls, in part by placing absolute caps on overall admissions and giving preference to the most readily assimilated races by developing a system of immigration quotas derived as percentages of census counts from idealized eras of the US past.

Congress acted upon these recommendations, first with the experimental 1921 Emergency Quota Act, and then permanently with the 1924 Johnson-Reed Immigration Act. This law banned outright the immigration of "aliens ineligible for citizenship," in an open rejection of Asians as inferior and unwelcome that immediately outraged the Japanese government. In the thick of World War II, Pearl Buck would testify before Congress that she believed the attack on Pearl Harbor stemmed from this egregious insult. The rest of the world received differential quotas produced as a percentage of each country's census population in the United States. By setting the baseline first in 1890, before the major surge of southern and eastern European immigration, and eventually back to 1790, this system aimed to maintain and restore an idealized racial composition for the nation. Great Britain and Northern Ireland received the largest quota at 65,721 per year, Germany was next at 25,957, then the Irish Free State at 17,853.

The most restrictive impact fell upon eastern and southern Europeans, who had been arriving in the greatest numbers since the 1880s. For example, Italians received an annual quota of 5,802, although the numbers of entries had ranged well above 100,000 per year since 1910. Enforcement of these regulations fell to US consulates, which held great discretionary power over the issuing of visas required for entry. This system of remote control operated more effectively than determining admissibility after migrants had already arrived on US shores at immigration centers such as Ellis Island or Angel Island. The law worked as intended immediately. Under the quota system, overall immigration was reduced to but a fraction of the peaks reached during the 1890s through the 1910s. Recorded immigration from Europe dropped from 364,339 in 1924 to 148,366 the following year, and averaged 160,000 the next four. After the 1920s, the chief problem of unwanted immigration became that of unsanctioned crossings across the United States' extensive land borders, particularly by Mexicans.

The national origins system quantified American welcome and hostility to people from all other parts of the world, as defined by their national origin, which at the time was considered to be congruent with racial types. Traditional allies had large quotas which affirmed migrations dating to the colonial era, whereas so-called new stock migrations had low quotas that reflected beliefs in the degree of their incompatibility with US values and civilization. The 1924 Immigration Law also institutionalized the view that Asians were utterly foreign, unassimilable, and therefore inadmissible. The Japanese government was infuriated at this absolute bar, as were countries with small quotas that had at least retained some entry rights. The national origins quota system and the racial restrictions on citizenship remained severe barriers to American efforts to cultivate friendships in vast expanses of the excluded and restricted world, until they were dismantled with the sweeping reforms of the 1965 Immigration Act. For the next four decades, however, this racially essentialist set of priorities predominated in US immigration policy.

As US nationals, Filipinos were among the last Asians to retain legal rights of entry into the United States and attract the attention of exclusionists as the "third Asiatic invasion." Little could or would be done about the other main groups—the small numbers of specified temporary visitors such as students, diplomats, merchants, tourists, and American-born Asians who held US citizenship, even when used to commit immigration fraud. The Immigration Bureau deployed its considerable powers of detention, surveillance, and interrogation to combat the "paper son" system, a daunting array of barriers which sharply limited the numbers seeking admission but largely failed to distinguish genuine from illegal entries. In contrast to this intractable enforcement problem, Congress *could* act to impose legal restrictions upon Filipinos.

By the 1930s, approximately fifty thousand Filipinos had made their way to the US mainland from Hawaii and directly from the Philippines. The earliest had sparked few anxieties as a trickle of government-sponsored students known as *pensionados*. With the official end of the Filipino-American War in 1902, the Philippine Commission, under the leadership of future US president William Howard Taft, decided to cultivate a corps of US-educated Filipino leaders and administrators to eventually assume authority, in part to legitimate US colonization as a civilizing mission. Between 1903 and 1914, 289 carefully selected *pensionadoes* drawn from many areas of the seven-thousand-island archipelago journeyed to the United States, where they attended high schools and then universities. In 1904, some of the *pensionados* made uncomfortable and highly contradictory appearances in the Philippine Exhibit at the St. Louis World's Fair as part of another diverse assortment of over a thousand Filipinos that included Tagalogs, Visayans, Muslims, Igorots, Tinguianes, Pampangans, Kalingas, Mangyans, Negritos, and Bagobos. Undermining the *pensionados'* concerted efforts to demonstrate Filipino capacities for modernity and Western civilization, the Fair's most popular feature was the performance of Filipino barbarity, particularly that of the headhunting, dog-eating Igorots wearing scanty "native" costumes, who underscored Filipino needs for American help. Upon returning to the Philippines, the *pensionadoes* attained prominent positions in government, education, engineering, law, medicine, and agriculture and led the campaigns for Philippine independence, holding themselves up as proof that Filipinos had become capable of self-government and that US supervision was no longer necessary.

Most Filipinos in the United States, however, wound up in the prosaic and often backbreaking struggle simply to survive. As late arrivals with few options but migrant labor in farms, fisheries, and canneries and no diplomatic representation, Filipinos inhabited a predominantly bachelor society strongly associated with all the presumed attending vices of itinerancy, poor character, gambling, lack of capital accumulation, and miscegenation. The Great Depression exacerbated nativist antagonisms with repressive and segregationist practices already institutionalized. Resentments against labor competition merged with long-simmering anger against the courtship of white women by brown men, boiling over with the 1930 Watsonville riots, which began at a taxi dance hall and raged for a week, eventually spreading to other towns in California's agricultural Central Valley. Such racialized tensions fueled pressure for an end to Filipino migration. However, to bar or limit the coming of Filipinos, the United States would have to grant its colony independence, so that its people could be treated as foreign subjects, a goal accomplished with the 1934 Tydings-McDuffie Act.

This willing contraction of American empire stemmed from long-standing tensions about whether and how the United States interacted with Asian peoples and states. From the start, anti-imperialists had objected to the extension of US territorial claims across the Pacific as violating the self-determination of Filipinos. Imperialists had justified this imposition of US authority as a civilizing project that would train and prepare Filipinos to govern themselves, a stage that Filipino independence activists claimed they had already attained. Although agricultural sectors pressed for continued access to Filipino workers, the dairy and cottonseed oil industries protested against imports of coconut oil and copra. The economic destitutions of the 1930s pressed the balance toward restriction and Filipinos gained the pledge of eventual independence. The creation of the Philippine Commonwealth greatly favored the interests of the United States, which supervised the writing of its constitution, and retained access to military bases and naval personnel, the right to apply tariffs, and restrict immigration. Filipinos received an annual entry quota of fifty. The Filipino Repatriation Act of 1935 sought to complete the elimination of the Filipino presence from the United States, although few took up the offer of one-way trips home.

A scant century after the arrival of the Siamese twins, cornerstones of their successful integration into American lives had become illegal and unavailable to later Asian immigrants: entry; citizenship; property ownership; and mixed-race marriage. The United States gates had closed as fully as practical against immigration from Asia, expressing an ideological vision of the American nation that nonetheless did not prevent Asians from finding ways of entering the United States, often under the duress of fraudulent or unsanctioned entry, and pursuing employment and other ways to support themselves and their dependents and establish stable lives.

Chapter 3
Living in the margins

In October 1926, the unmarried eighteen-year-old *Nisei* Ishikawa Suetsugu leased a berry and vegetable farm in Mountain View, California. Ishikawa was not being precocious, but simply enacting a family strategy to help his *issei* parents claim a precarious foothold in the United States, despite the considerable barriers presented by the Alien Land Laws. The eldest of five children, Suetsugu was the first in his family to hold US citizenship, and he arranged the farming leasehold as soon as he became a legal adult in order to secure some stability and scope for savings. Through their US-born son, the Ishikawas fared better than the many other Japanese American farmers who were never able to gain stable access to farmland, an economic investment that required several years of cultivation before producing profits. Instead, they remained trapped as sharecroppers or transient laborers. In contrast, the Ishikawas succeeded through their efforts as a family unit. Suetsugu married and continued living with his parents, along with his wife Tsugiyo. Nonetheless, they had to work for twenty-five years before they had saved up enough to buy a forty-acre farm outright.

Other *issei* were not fortunate enough to have citizen children. Sometimes, Suetsugu helped childless *issei* by using his status to lease land on their behalf. Even Japanese American families with children resorted to such tactics. Kanemoto Hatsu, the eldest of twelve children, was born in 1916, too late to attain adulthood before the 1920 Alien Land Law would have forced her *issei* parents to relinquish their farm. Instead, her family leased land through a *Nisei* acquaintance, whose brother, Yoshito, Hatsu later married. Like Hatsu, most *Nisei* were born during the 1910s and did not become old enough to lease or buy land until the 1930s. Birthright citizenship was a key stepping stone to securing rights in the United States, although the status still did not protect the American-born from racial discrimination in the United States.

Asians who immigrated earlier—before passage of laws intended to drive them away by severely limiting their employment options—were able to manage the hostilities better. Such was the case of Sakauye Eiichi, the eldest of seven children whose *issei* father managed to buy a farm in 1907 before enactment of the 1913 Alien Land Law. Despite the intensifying discrimination in legal and economic practices, the Great Depression of the 1920s, and the wholesale removal of Japanese Americans as "enemy aliens" from the West Coast during World War II, the Sakauyes would manage to hold onto their piece of America and eventually reclaim their lives there.

Exclusion (1882–1952) stemmed from widely held beliefs in the inferiority and unassimilability of Asians as a biologically distinct race. General acceptance of the "sciences" of Social Darwinism and eugenics—which advocated selective breeding and reproduction to develop superior human populations—justified discriminations such as immigration controls, bans on naturalized citizenship, limits on economic options and political participation, and a host of other segregationist measures. As the first targets of immigration restrictions and the accompanying enforcement mechanisms, the Chinese American population reached an exclusion-era peak at 118,746 in 1900, after which more effective border controls reduced their numbers through the 1920s, when increases through native births started overtaking deaths and departures to replenish numbers. The terms of the 1907

Gentlemen's Agreement allowed the Japanese American population to continue growing (particularly through the immigration of women who produced children), and overtake the ranks of Chinese by 1910 to reach 152,745. This comparatively greater gender balance survived even the 1920 ending of picture-bride immigration and the absolute ban of 1924, as Japanese remained the community with the greatest ability to expand through families through the 1970s. In 1920, Japanese America included about 30,000 *Nisei*, a number that grew to 68,000 over the next decade. Filipinos were the third major Asian group to arrive, with migration waxing during the 1920s to reach a population high of 108,424 in 1930, before waning with passage of the 1934 Tydings-McDuffie Act. These successive waves of Asian immigration occupied similar economic niches, but with shrinking opportunities over time as segregationist measures gained effectiveness.

Asian Americans remained primarily associated with demarcated residential and employment niches that confined their threat to whites, but also facilitated the pooling and sharing of resources necessary for survival in an openly hostile society. Although ideologically and legally all Asians were similarly positioned as outsiders to the United States, the label "Asian American" was something of a misnomer, because Asian immigrants identified most strongly with those sharing their nationality and native place, not as a multiethnic group. Ethnic Asian American communities emerged as structured around networks and associations most often rooted in kinship, shared native-place and dialect, employment, and homeland politics that did not always have as their object the United States. The marginality of Asian American existences during this era led many by necessity to adopt open minds about their future options. Even as Asian Americans struggled and sometimes succeeded to sink roots in an unwelcoming United States, they also bore in mind the reality that returning home or migrating elsewhere might be a better option, or even a necessity. World War II both clarified and reworked this balance of competing realities, in part by justifying the fullest implementation of Asian racialized segregation with the incarceration of Japanese Americans as "enemy aliens," but also by forcing a reconsideration of American democratic ideals and the entwining of foreign relations with immigration restrictions to mandate improved possibilities and conditions for Asian inclusion into the United States.

Families and ethnic Americans

Under the legal and economic constraints of exclusion, Asian American communities were overwhelmingly male, as only the wealthier or more fortunate were able to marry and have children. Gender imbalances persisted through the 1970s, particularly for Chinese and Filipinos, and despite modest shifts in immigration laws, which permitted greater rights of family reunification between World War II and 1965. Japanese and Korean communities had relatively more women, due to picture-bride immigration. In 1910, 85 percent of Japanese immigrants were male, but more women arrived between 1908 and 1920, so that the gender ratio dropped from six men for each woman to just under two men per woman in 1920.

In contrast, Chinese American men outnumbered women 14 to 1 in 1910, and 7 to 1 in 1920. Chinese, if possessed of the resources, also sought brides from China, although this kind of marriage required a journey back home. The greater costs and uncertainties of life in the United States led many men, such as both Doc Ing Hay and Lung On of John Day, Oregon, to leave their wives in China. During the 1920s and 1930s, an estimated 25 to 40 percent of seemingly bachelor Chinese were actually married with families they supported back in their home villages. Such long-distance family practices characterized many Asian Americans, who remitted considerable funds to immediate and distant relatives, and to support charitable and community causes, thereby signaling their strong sense of native-place obligations and possible, eventual return. As long as the United States remained so unwelcoming, the option of departure remained open for many, even for the US-born.

The imbalance in gender ratios severely limited marriage options in the United States. Moreover, anti-miscegenation laws (California's dated back to 1880 and remained on the books until 1948) forbade white marriages to "Negro, mulatto, and Mongolian" persons. Asian women in America tended to be highly pursued, as the main alternative to marrying one of them was to marry a prospect from home. For those unable or disinclined to travel, proximity of residence, recreation sites, and workplaces, along with irregular enforcement of anti-miscegenation laws by local city clerks, shaped marriage markets. In California's Imperial Valley bordering Mexico, Punjabi men met and married Mexican women whose fathers and brothers they worked with in the fields. Filipinos courted and intermarried white, Native American, Japanese, and Chinese women, incurring great resentments. In Mississippi, Chinese storekeepers mingled with the African American community. Chinese marriages to white women were more feasible on the East Coast, which did not have as many prohibitions. The educator Yung Wing and his younger relative Yung Kwai both married white, New England women. New York had no anti-miscegenation laws and so as early as 1840, Chinese men had been marrying Irish women whom they met while working together in domestic and laundry services—a phenomenon visible enough to feature in late nineteenth-century song lyrics and vaudeville acts such as "The Heathen Chinee Waltz" (1871) or "The Coon and the Chink" (1912).

These limited options for traditional family lives with wives and children underscores the reality that, due to legal and economic circumstances, many Asian Americans during the exclusion era were single, laboring-class men of working age. For example, in 1930, 97 percent of Filipinos in Santa Clara County were male, and 78 percent were between the ages of eighteen and thirty. Patterns of labor recruitment and exclusionary laws produced an average age for Filipinos of twenty-seven for adult males, much younger than the average age of Chinese and Japanese in the county, which were thirty-seven and forty, respectively. Eighty percent of Filipinos were single, compared to 48 percent of Chinese and 39 percent of Japanese. For many of these men, fraternity and friendship provided the most intimate bonds, although they also appeared to be antisocial and irresponsible forms of social organization which exacerbated concerns regarding the unassimilability of Asians, as in the case of Chinese sworn brotherhoods, which were also known as secret societies or tongs and associated with crime and vice industries.

On the West Coast, even bicultural, middle-class Asian American families faced racial restrictions that prevented their integration into mainstream economic and social circles, as demonstrated by the highly acculturated Joseph (1852–1935) and Mary Tape (1857–1934). Both were born in China but came to San Francisco separately as orphans raised by missionary organizations. They learned English, became Christian, and aspired for futures in the United States. After working as a houseboy, Joseph gained employment delivering milk and then as a drayman. He cut off his queue by the early 1870s, signaling his decision to remain in the United States. The two married in a wedding attended by the Leland Stanfords (the founders of the famed university) in 1875 and presided over by the leading Chinatown missionary, the Reverend A. W. Loomis. Joseph prospered as a bilingual Chinese American who provided crucial connective services between less acculturated Chinese and mainstream society. From his office on Dupont Street (now Grant Avenue) in Chinatown, Joseph developed a monopoly on bonding and transporting bonded Chinese (a necessary service for Chinese ships' crew members) and handled large drayage contracts for wholesale Chinese merchants while interpreting for the Chinese Consulate in San Francisco. He later became the first Chinese passenger agent and bonds-broker for the Pacific Mail and the Southern Pacific Railroad, and engaged in myriad other kinds of brokering work related to the business of migration.

The Tapes lived outside of Chinatown and ran into problems when they sought to enroll their eldest daughter, Mamie, in the local Spring Valley primary school. Recent California state legislation had provided for the education of "all children" without specification of race. However, the school's principal turned Mamie away as Chinese, instigating the Tapes to sue. The case of *Tape v. Hurley* (1886) won at each level of court proceedings including the California Supreme Court, thereby judicially verifying the rights of Chinese to attend public schools. However, Mamie never attended an integrated school, because the California State legislature quickly passed new legislation creating separate schools for "Mongolian or Chinese" children—thus setting a major precedent for the 1896 Supreme Court decision, *Plessy v. Ferguson*, which famously found that "separate but equal" facilities were constitutional. The Tape children attended the Oriental School in Chinatown until they moved to Berkeley, where the younger Tape children attended integrated schools.

Although they lived in Chinatown only a few years, the Tapes remained bound to serving as brokers between the Chinese enclave and the American mainstream. The thoroughly bicultural Tapes grew affluent from their employment and business activities as intermediaries, even as they could not escape their racialization as Chinese. As brokers, they benefited from the segregation that they could not themselves fully escape, and thus occupied morally ambiguous positions as both gatekeepers and facilitators who both protested and profited from the discrimination against fellow Chinese. Many ethnic communities featured brokers—for example, the Italian padrone or the Irish ward boss—but among Euro-American ethnic groups brokers became less necessary with integrating second generations, something largely beyond the purview of even US-born Asian Americans. Even Mamie and her siblings remained bound to the Chinese American community, with all three Tape daughters marrying Chinese Americans. In 1904, their brother Frank and Mamie's husband Herman Lowe were among the first ethnic Chinese to obtain jobs as interpreters for the Immigration Bureau. Their American-born brother-in-law Robert Park was another pioneer in attaining this kind of government position, which required high levels of trust; he also helped to found the Chinese American Citizens Alliance.

The extension of such racialized constraints even to American-born generations fostered transnational attachments to ancestral homelands. Despite significant educational and organizational achievements demonstrating their capacities for high levels of acculturation, US-born Chinese shared their immigrant parents' understanding that better opportunities existed in societies without such institutionalized anti-Asian beliefs. *Nisei* Kanemoto Hatsu recalled that during the 1920s her teachers respected Japanese American children as hard-working, industrious, studious, and clean and compared them favorably with southern European and Mexican classmates. Despite academic attainments, however, Asian American students were segregated from school clubs and extracurricular activities. Even at the college and university level, US-born Chinese interacted chiefly with their international student counterparts, whom they occasionally married, as in the cases of Flora Belle Jan and Rose Hum Lee. Neither marriage was successful, indicating that shared heritage did not guarantee marital compatibility.

The degree of Chinese American orientation to China is revealed by a 1935 survey conducted at a Chinese Young People's conference held in Lake Tahoe. The gathering included highly acculturated youth, most of whom were Christian and most likely college-educated. Of this select group, 75 percent favored a future in China. In 1936 the Ging Hawk Club in New York sponsored a national essay competition entitled, "Does my Future Lie in China or America?" A great outcry ensued at the first-prize essay, by Robert Dunn, who was raised in Roxbury, Massachusetts and attended Harvard University, which began, "In America lies my future." Many more Chinese American youth agreed with the second-prize essay, by Kaye Hong, a University of Washington student, who asserted, "The old adage, 'Go west, young man' no longer becomes applicable to this American youth... It is for me, 'Go further west, young man.' Yes, further west, across the Pacific to China." In China, many believed they would be able to actively support their homeland's quest for modernization and rejuvenation and find gainful employment in professional and white-collar jobs.

Nisei also fostered significant orientations to Japan. In 1935, of the 186,850 *Nisei* counted by the Japanese consulate in the United States and Hawaii, close to forty thousand had spent some time in Japan, ranging from studies of several years, short stays such as summer visits and study tours, or university attendance, with thirteen to fourteen thousand never returning to the United States. Of the approximately twenty-four thousand who did, about half (12,338) had spent eight to nine years in Japan. Sent by their overworked parents drawn by access to cheaper education, *Nisei* also saw advantages to remaining in Japan. During the late 1920s, the Japanese Foreign Ministry's Commercial Division surveyed *Nisei* in Japan and found that three-fourths of those from the continental United States and 90 percent from Hawaii preferred Japan to returning home. Some explained this preference by pointing out that university-credentialed *kibei* had returned, only to find jobs as migrant farm labor in the United States. Some migrated elsewhere within the Japanese empire to new opportunities in Manchuria. Many identified with Japan's imperialist successes which they defended when back in the United States, inspired in part by the sense of racial identification and acceptance they had experienced and which they were denied in the United States.

Many *kibei*, in fact, felt marginalized in both the United States and Japan and organized their own groups within the larger *Nisei* community in order to articulate their own political concerns. As relative newcomers, often *kibei* were more working-class and had less access to business and farm ownership. They tended to be laborers on the farms run by fellow *Nisei* who had remained in the United States, setting down roots.

Livelihoods

Anti-Asian hostilities became institutionalized through laws, government bureaucracies, and social and economic discrimination. Nonetheless, Asian Americans continued to carve out lives and livelihoods within a shrinking arena of opportunities. To negotiate and survive, the predominantly male populations of Asian Americans occupied less contested economic niches such as international trade, service industries, manual labor, and agriculture—but they also developed new types of businesses from their marginalized status: professional services that drew on the networks facilitating migration and employment; and businesses plying tourism and international trade.

Leadership for Asian ethnic communities arose among the wealthiest and most influential individuals, who were primarily engaged in businesses such as import-export trade, newspapers, large-scale agriculture, labor recruiting, and merchandizing. Such business leaders often served as intermediaries between ethnic Asian communities and mainstream society (much like the Tapes of San Francisco), because they had the English-language skills to develop bicultural relationships, along with the financial wherewithal, widespread networks, and entrepreneurial acumen to identify and develop new economic possibilities.

Bengali Muslim traders illustrate this ingenuity and multicultural adaptability. During the 1880s, they began bringing embroidered silks and other "exotic" goods, to cater to the prevailing fashion for "Indian" and "Oriental" goods. After arriving in the United States, usually in New York, they pursued this trade by following American leisure travelers and consumers from the beach boardwalks of New Jersey, and then to tourist destinations in the south, the Caribbean, and Central America, peddling embroidered goods such as silk and cotton handkerchiefs, bedspreads, pillow covers, and tablecloths. Their business linked wives in West Bengal villages, who manufactured the embroidered goods and tended farms, to wives in the United States, usually from black and Creole communities in places such as Harlem and Tremé in New Orleans, who anchored the trade in the United States. During the 1917–1918 season, Bengali traders plied their business in New Orleans, Charleston, Memphis, Chattanooga, Galveston, Dallas, Birmingham, Atlanta, and Jacksonville. Although numbering only a few hundred in any one decade through the 1920s, their circulations reflect broader patterns of the high mobility of Asians pursuing scattered economic opportunities within the United States and their reliance on transnational networks and family organizations, as well as the emerging marketing of ethnic goods and culture.

Far more Asians, however, were laborers, usually employed in agriculture. When Kawahara Katsusaburo arrived in San Jose in 1911 as a child joining his immigrant parents, he recalled that Japanese Americans were mostly "hard-working young people in their thirties," young men without families or older people. About 130,000 free laborers left rural Japan for the US continent and Hawaii between 1895 and 1908, usually as single men or without their wives, as did most Asian immigrants during this era.

Japanese had turned to rural labor with their earliest arrivals on the continental United States in the 1880s. By the 1890s they had started replacing aging Chinese workers, whose ranks were diminishing due to the Chinese exclusion laws. In 1900, 40 percent of Japanese in Santa Clara County worked in agriculture, and 95 percent as laborers. In contrast, 61 percent of Chinese worked in farming, and 89 percent as laborers. By 1915, an estimated 50 to 60 percent of all Japanese immigrants on the US mainland were engaged in agriculture with laborers following the crops: strawberries from April through June; harvesting apricots, pears, prunes in July and August; then late summer in Fresno to pick grapes. All Asian farm laborers faced clustering in backbreaking "stoop" or "squat" labor such as weeding, thinning, hoeing, and picking berries and asparagus; and topping and loading sugar beets.

In 1909, Japanese workers were distributed as follows: agriculture was the biggest employer at upwards of 38,000, with 30,000 working in California; 10,000 employed by railroad companies throughout the west; 2,200 in sawmills in Oregon and Washington; about 3,600 in salmon canneries in Alaska, Oregon, and Washington, with only a few hundred in the fishing industry; and about 2,000 miners in Wyoming, Utah, and Colorado. A further 22,000 to 26,000 Japanese were in urban service trades or in small businesses such as restaurants, boarding houses, hotels, and barbershops.

Across ethnic lines, male Asian laborers followed a range of jobs through the seasons up and down the West Coast, with Chinese, Japanese, Koreans, Indians, and Filipinos located in similar occupational niches in agriculture, lumberyards, fishing and canneries, and service. Chinese, Japanese, and Filipino students alike sought to fund their studies while working as household domestics, with varying degrees of success. For Asians living in Los Angeles during the 1930s, work as movie extras provided higher daily wages; they served as background in popular movie serials featuring caricatures drawn from literature such as the evil Fu Manchu, the obsequious Charlie Chan, and the suffering peasants of the epic *The Good Earth*, based on Pearl Buck's Pulitzer Prize winning novel. Asian Americans shared workplaces and frequented each other's businesses, although often on unequal and sometimes tense terms, particularly as earlier arrivals enjoyed greater capacities to establish businesses in ways that limited opportunities for latecomers.

In response to the hostilities producing the Gentlemen's Agreement, Japanese Americans had turned to farming to mitigate anti-Asian racism under the strong encouragement of leaders such as Abiko Kyutaro and George Shima and Japanese diplomatic representatives, who also urged Japanese Americans to display desirable cultural values by starting families. Although they nonetheless attracted white hostility, Japanese American farm owners gained greater status and economic stability as the percentage of laborers in the workforce shrank from 95 percent in 1900 to 79 percent in 1910, with 20.5 percent leasing or owning their own farms. In comparison, the ratio of Chinese laborers to farmers remained constant over the same years. Kawahara Katsusaburo's family was able to lease land starting in 1921; Kawahara became a celery specialist who was able to steadily increase his holdings from 40 acres to 80 in 1927, and then 225 acres at the beginning of World War II. Kawahara hired workers through Asian labor recruiters; at first, these were Japanese, and later Filipinos, for whom he provided housing, although they were responsible for their own meals.

As the last major group to arrive, Filipinos faced the fewest options for establishing themselves, and were confined mostly to unskilled jobs alongside small numbers of self-supporting students and naval-service veterans. Chinese and Japanese already occupied business niches and other positions of influence and greater profitability. For example, when Filipinos entered the fish-processing industries of the Pacific Northwest and Alaska in 1921, the labor recruiters were Chinese and Japanese; and only later did some Filipinos attain such established positions. After the *pensionadoes*, about two thousand laborers arrived on the mainland in 1923, mostly re-migrating from Hawaii. With the end of Japanese migration in 1924, more direct routes from Manila brought Filipinos to Pacific-coast ports such as Los Angeles, San Francisco, and Seattle as a replacement workforce. Like Chinese and Japanese before them, Filipinos skewed young and male and by 1930, 94 percent of the more than 45,000 Filipinos on the mainland were men, with 67 percent in California. The writer and labor organizer Carlos Bulosan shared the labor and desperation of fellow Filipinos struggling through the depressed conditions of the 1930s, movingly describing their frustrated hopes and suffering in his fictionalized, composite biography, *America is in the Heart* (1943): "I came to know that in many ways it was a crime to be Filipino in California... I feel like a criminal running away from a crime I did not commit. And this crime is that I am a Filipino in America."

Eighty percent of Filipinos on the Pacific coast were migratory workers who annually followed agricultural schedules to journey through Delano and Fresno in California to harvest grapes, Salinas to pick lettuce, and Stockton to harvest asparagus. Some including students went to Alaska during the summers to work in the salmon-canning industry which paid higher wages and offered better living conditions than camps and barracks in the field, but required repetitive and dangerous work. During winters, some congregated in urban centers to work in service industries. In 1930, an estimated 11,441 Filipinos in California worked in service occupations as houseboys, chauffeurs, bellboys, kitchen helpers, dishwashers, busboys, or in some combination in hotels and restaurants.

From Gold Rush times, Chinese and Asians filled the steady need for domestic service, whether as household servants, in laundries, or in restaurants. Despite segregationist fears of racial mixing, Asian men, whether Chinese, Japanese, or Filipinos, readily found employment as household domestics: cooks, houseboys, and fountain-pen boys (aspiring Filipino students during the 1920s and 1930s) who worked to support their studies. The cleaver-wielding cook, Hop Sing, of the long-running television show *Bonanza*, captured the quasi-familial status some could attain through long service, although many hoped such employment would be a steppingstone to cover educational costs on the way to better opportunities. As early as 1851, Chinese opened laundries, which became geographically dispersed throughout urban areas in the United States, by undertaking this particularly onerous household chore before the age of washing machines and dryers. Restaurants, associated with cheap and tasty food, was another labor-intensive, daily necessity that middle-class households willingly relinquished to Chinese and Japanese. These forms of business provided stable employment that required few initial skills and minimal start-up capital.

5. These formally arrayed young Filipino men belonged to Caballeros de Dimas-Alang in Seattle, about 1935. This fraternal order promoted independence in the Philippines while providing camaraderie and mutual aid in the United States for the predominantly male, working-age Filipino American population.

Businessmen operating diverse projects constituted the backbone of Asian American communities, in part because they provided the essential connective tissue linking their poorer co-ethnics in the United States to mainstream society and its economic and political structures, as well as to homeland responsibilities and organizations. Among Japanese, Abiko and Shima were prominent examples, with their significant roles in newspapers, labor recruiting, farming cooperatives, the Japanese Association of America, collaborations with the Japanese government, and lobbying efforts and stewardship of legal campaigns in the United States. Chen Yixi (Chin Gee Hee, 1844–1929) made his fortune as a labor recruiter, railroad engineer, and import-export trader. Chen arrived as a teenager, learned English, and made many strategic contacts in his ascent from laborer to major business figure in Seattle who worked closely with Anglo counterparts while representing Chinese interests. Through his close ties to local leaders, including Mayor Henry Yesler and the lawyer Thomas Burke, Chen remained in Seattle even in the thick of the expulsions of Chinese in 1885–1886; just a few years later, he constructed one of Seattle's first brick buildings, the block-long Kong Yick Building, in 1889. With legal advice from Burke and channeling complaints through the Chinese consulate, Chen helped Chinese receive $700,000 for their damages—a rare instance of reparations for anti-Asian violence in the nineteenth century.

Asian American businessmen facilitated trade and other forms of economic cooperation between their homelands and emerging centers for trans-Pacific trade on the West Coast. In Seattle, Chen Yixi recruited Chinese laborers who constructed the Northern Pacific Railroad and the Burke Building, thereby earning the gratitude and friendship of key Seattle boosters such as James J. Hill and Burke, as did Charles Tetsuo Takahashi and Furuya Masajiro, who recruited Japanese workers. Such businessmen identified and made the connections needed to develop Asian markets for American goods such as rice, wheat, lumber, and dried seafood, while arranging Asian imports such as workers, curios, groceries, and other sundries consumed by Asian Americans. On the Chinese end, Hong Kong became the key port with specialized import-export businesses known as Gold Mountain firms or *jinshanzhuang*, which focused on trans-Pacific transactions. Migration provided manifold business opportunities to provide travel arrangements, mail services and remittances to hinterland villages, paper identities to evade the exclusion laws, trade in goods such as dried and canned foods, clothing, printed media, daily hardware, herbal medicines, temporary housing, and investment services. Merchants also played key leadership roles. During the mid-1880s, the merchant-led Chinese Consolidated Benevolent Association (CCBA) hired lawyers to challenge discriminatory local ordinances and led the unsuccessful campaign to have the 1892 Geary Act declared unconstitutional; the CCBA also facilitated building of the Chinese hospital in 1925.

Away from major enclaves, Asian businesses in smaller communities could become more integrated in serving both Asian and non-Asian customers. In John Day, Oregon, the Kam Wah Chung Company served fellow Chinese as a clearinghouse for goods, services, information, and networks as well as a local social and supply center, post office, labor-contracting office, and medicinal herb shop with shelves stocked with many Chinese goods including medicines, sandalwood fans, and ginseng. The business also served non-Chinese customers by selling general goods such as candy, tobacco, matches, firecrackers, beer, and incense, along with staples such as soaps, coffees, candles, lard, canned goods, sugar, flour, cotton, and rice, and handling mail orders. Starting in the 1870s, Chinese in Southern states such as Mississippi, Louisiana, and parts of Tennessee and Arkansas ran grocery stores whose chief customers were African Americans, who were unwelcome in white-owned businesses.

Perhaps more than in any other ethnic Asian community, Chinese American business leaders in Chinatowns such as San Francisco, New York, and Los Angeles cultivated non-Chinese tourism alongside providing essential goods and services for Chinese. For the mobile, male, working-classes and local residents, Chinatowns provided associational contacts, residences, postal and financial services, restaurants, import-export stores, and groceries, as well as recreational venues such as theaters, gambling halls, brothels, and opium dens. After the 1890s, they also catered to a significant customer base of non-Chinese seeking exotic thrills. The 1906 San Francisco earthquake and fire destroyed all of Chinatown except for the brick St. Mary's Church, giving Chinese American business leaders an opportunity to rebuild in ways that fostered ethnic forms of belonging in the United States.

Although some Anglo business leaders considered using the tragedy to dislodge Chinatown from its strategic downtown location, Chinese American merchant leaders persuaded them of the greater advantages of keeping it in place. They rebuilt Chinatown with enhanced tourist appeal, featuring ornately decorated buildings, housing, restaurants, curio and antique stores; dragon-festooned streetlamps; elaborate balconies and rooftops; competing pagoda towers at the corners of Grant and California streets; bars and nightclubs; and a telephone exchange designed to look like a Confucian temple. Through deliberate self-exoticization, inexpensive but tasty Chinese American foods, and cheaply made imports, Chinatown marketed for the curiosity of outsiders an artificial version of Chinese American culture, which nonetheless provided significant profits. Ornate gates inscribed with four character phrases prominently marked such conversions to consumer tastes.

The link to orientalist fantasy is perhaps most clear in the brief existence of Los Angeles' China City, which was constructed from movie sets recycled from the 1937 epic *The Good Earth*. By the 1920s, San Francisco's Chinatown had become its second-most-popular tourist attraction after Golden Gate Park. The earthquake's destruction of city records provided another less visible, but nonetheless critical, inroad in destroying birth and marriage records so that tens of thousands of Chinese men could claim birth in San Francisco and thereby *jus solis* citizenship, derived from place of birth—the basis for the "paper son" immigration fraud system that so perniciously undermined the intent of the exclusion laws.

Little Tokyos or Japantowns (*Nihonmachis*) sprang up as the community gained a certain measure of affluence and stability. Japanese started settling in Seattle during the economic boom that came with completion of the Great Northern Railway in 1896.

The railroad magnate James J. Hill was transforming Seattle into a central node for trans-Pacific trade and arranged for the Nippon Yusen Kaisha to choose it as the eastern nexus of its northern shipping route, beating out San Diego.

The numbers of both Chinese and Japanese increased steadily, with the timing of the latter's arrival positioning Japanese to benefit from the ensuing period of growth. Pan-ethnic residential and business districts developed south of Yesler Way with high concentrations of Japanese in business. Prominent Japanese American Seattle residents such as Furuya Masajiro (1862–1938) struck it rich through international and diverse businesses including wholesale and retail import-export, banking, labor contracting, and mail delivery, but most clustered in small businesses. A 1924 survey found 1,920 businesses: 1,462 owned by Japanese with 46 percent in small businesses, compared to the national average of 5 percent. Japanese Americans were only 2.8 percent of the city's population, but they operated 26 percent of the hotels, 23 percent of barbershops, and 26 percent of dye works and cleaning businesses. From 1900 until 1925, those running hotels and boarding houses increased from only 3 hotels and rooming houses to 127—a lifestyle invoked in Monica Sone's memoir, *Nisei Daughter* (1953). From World War I through the 1930s, Japanese Americans ran 70 percent of the stalls in Pike Place Market in Seattle. The Japanese Commercial Club and the Japanese Chamber of Commerce promoted Japanese-owned businesses by regulating competition, promoting mutual assistance, and sharing information.

Unlike Chinese and Japanese, Filipinos struggled more to establish commercial districts. Their high levels of mobility required, in the words of Linda Espana-Maram, "networks of portable communities," although during the off season Filipinos generally returned to Little Manilas which featured smaller numbers of businesses such as restaurants, barbershops, pool halls, and entertainment centers. The late timing of their arrival,

6. This undated postcard depicts San Francisco's Chinatown's Grant Avenue, the key tourist area in which residents pursued their everyday shopping surrounded by the ornate, elaborately orientalist architecture, signage, and lampposts.

during the 1920s, meant that there were few US-born to help them claim property, and so the working-class men lived in cheap hotels and experienced working-class lifestyles. To a greater degree than Chinatowns and *Nihonmachis*, Little Manilas experienced seasonal fluctuations in their populations. In Stockton, for example, winter residents shrank to about three thousand but grew to more than eight thousand during the growing and harvesting seasons of spring and summer. Even such mobile and dispersed communities managed nonetheless to arrange their communities in associations promoting circles of shared interests.

Associational life

More so than European immigrants who, despite ethnic differences, could eventually claim the legal and economic privileges of whiteness, Asian immigrants relied upon networks and cooperation with co-ethnics for survival under hostile circumstances. In the absence of families, for many of the men compatriotism, religion, employment, and fraternal loyalties and shared interests assumed great importance. Various systems of values and codes of ethics mandated such mutual support. The Filipino system of aid was called *utang na loob*, which roughly translates as "an internal debt" and required family and kin group members to provide service, hospitality, and protection if possible, which had to be reciprocated for fear of incurring great shame. Chinese associations drew upon principles of shared surnames and native-place as well as traditions of sworn brotherhood. Japanese also drew upon native-place bonds, business and agricultural collaborations, education, recreation, and religion, which constituted major reasons for cooperative activities and bonds. Even as American-born generations staked out their communal lives, they remained segregated within the same racial boundaries that had restricted their parents' generation.

Newspapers articulated and mapped out competing interests and worldviews for ethnic Asian communities. As early as 1853, San Francisco's *Golden Hills News* was possibly the first Chinese-language newspaper published in the United States. Wong Chin Foo started the earliest Chinese-language newspaper published east of California, the weekly *Chinese American*, in 1883. The Christian reverend and public speaker Ng Poon Chew founded the *Chung Sai Yat Po* (Zhongxi ribao in Putonghua pronunciation, Chinese West Daily, 1900–1951) which competed for readers with *Sai Gai Yat Po* (Shijie ribao, Chinese World Daily, 1909–1969) which closely followed revolutionary events in China, particularly in support of Sun Yat-sen's Nationalist Party. Newspapers conveyed strong editorial perspectives, with Abiko Kyutaro using the San Francisco-based *Nichibei Shimbun* (founded 1899) to disseminate his Christian, acculturating vision for Japanese Americans, often in competition with the *Shin Sekai*, which tended to represent non-Christian, more working-class, Japanese American perspectives. In recognition of the emerging

Nisei generation, *Nichibei Shimbun* was the first to add an English-language section in 1925. Founded in 1903, the *Rafu Shimpo* (1903–1942) served the Los Angeles community until its demise with World War II. Also based in Los Angeles, the Philippine fraternal order Caballeros de Dimas-Alang published the English-language *Philippines Review* twice monthly across the 1920s, conveying news of the Philippines and its progress toward independence.

Newspapers captured the ebb and flow of community issues and affairs, not only in editorial and news sections but also in advertisements and literary sections. During the 1910s, for example, Japanese American newspapers frequently featured announcements from husbands seeking runaway wives, illustrating the common failure of arranged picture-bride marriages.

Newspapers provided forums for the sharing of news and opinion about conditions in the United States, but also served as vehicles for transnational engagements with homeland politics. Although they well understood American lobbying and legal procedures, Asian immigrants faced severe restrictions on their political involvement in the United States. Between 1906 and 1931, the Chinese Students Alliance, which included members from both China and the United States, published the *Chinese Students Monthly*, which commented on China's struggles for modernization, international relations, and discriminations against Chinese in the United States. The main Filipino organization, Caballeros de Dimas-Alang (founded 1906), evoked the pseudonym of martyred independence leader José Rizal to convey its mission to campaign for liberation from the United States. The first US branch was inaugurated in 1921 and expanded quickly to twenty-six lodges by the mid-1930s in California. Although its newspaper featured reporting on events in the Philippines, in the United States Caballeros adapted to the realities of its members' lives by changing the language of their activities from Tagalog to English to accommodate more members from the many regions represented at meetings; the organization also focused on providing assistance with food, clothing, and funds for medical and burial expenses. Mutual aid was a common feature of other Filipino associations, which included the Filipino Mercantile Association, Filipino Brotherhood Association, Filipino-American Christian Fellowship, and the umbrella Filipino Federation of America.

Independence for their colonized homelands also preoccupied the Korean and Indian communities. Many Koreans had migrated to the United States because conditions had become so difficult at home under Japanese rule. This exilic group enjoyed some support from the US government as an indirect criticism of Japan's expanding influence in the western Pacific. In 1913, the US Secretary of State tacitly supported Korean National Association leaders when they protested Japanese diplomatic claims to represent them after an outburst of anti-Korean violence in Hemet, California. Korean nationalist leaders established military-training bases in Manchuria, a provisional government in Shanghai in 1919, and mobilized Korean Americans to send money and support independence leaders.

The best known in the United States, Syngman Rhee, fled Korea in 1904 and became the first Korean to receive an American PhD, from Princeton, in 1910. He traveled widely, seeking international support for Korean independence, and lobbied constantly in Congress. In contrast, Indian independence activists, such as the Gadar Party founded by Har Dayal in 1913, faced repressive measures by the Canadian and US governments acting in support of the British. Indian revolutionaries also operated transnationally. For example, the Singapore-based businessman and Gadar Party-member Baba Gurdit Singh commissioned the Japanese ship *Komagata Maru* in 1914 to protest Canadian exclusionary laws. This effort failed through the collusion of the British-colonial and Canadian governments, which also worked with the United States in 1917 to crush an attempt by the Gadar Party to foment revolution by secretly returning home. American-provided intelligence enabled colonial authorities to meet and arrest the revolutionaries immediately upon arrival.

China also exiled its share of political rebels. Kang Youwei of the reformist Protect the Emperor Society raised awareness of his cause and recruited followers among American Chinese during the 1890s and 1900s, overshadowing for a time the now far-better-known Sun Yat-sen with his message of revolution and republican government. The Cantonese Sun Yat-sen fostered ties with the fraternal order Zhigongtang, which rallied US-based supporters to Sun's Nationalist Party and vision for democracy in China. The fall of the Qing in 1911 launched China into decades of political and social experimentation and upheaval in the quest for modernization and re-emergence as a world power, attracting considerable investment and involvement from Chinese Americans, for whom China's resurgence would surely enhance their status in the United States. The established and respected Japanese government, in contrast, worked with a largely compliant Japanese Association of America, despite rumblings and complaints when its international relations priorities prevented it from challenging the US government in matters pertaining to the living and working conditions of Japanese Americans.

Although they were usually perceived as unified racial groups, each Asian American community varied according to region, political orientation, class, and employment. For example, two different independence organizations competed for the loyalties of Korean Americans: Rhee's Korean Congress and Park Yong-man's Korean Military Corps. The Chinese American umbrella organization CCBA tended to emphasize the interests of its merchant leaders, to the detriment of working-class members. The most onerous constraint was the CCBA's arrangement with shipping companies, which stated that no Chinese could depart without its permission, signifying that all debts had been cleared. The CCBA's failure to duly represent the concerns of laundrymen inspired the founding of the Chinese Hand Laundry Alliance in

1933, which began publishing the *China Daily News* in 1940 to address working-class issues.

Labor organizing was perhaps the most relevant associational principle among Filipino Americans. By the mid-1920s in California, Filipino farm workers were 42 percent of all nonwhite, unskilled workers in the fields. This high visibility attracted the brunt of antagonism; Filipino farm workers were seen as displacing white workers and lowering wage scales. Filipinos began organizing at smaller levels but did not attain any broader impact until the Filipino Labor Union (FLU) formed in 1933, and oversaw a strike of seven hundred lettuce pickers, who walked off the fields in Salinas Valley. The strike—which ended with violence—failed but nevertheless demonstrated the FLU's capacities to organize actions. In 1934 the FLU had over two thousand members and joined with the Vegetable Packers Association—a mostly white union chartered with the American Federation of Labor (AFL)—in a work stoppage in Monterey County. Under attack by the law officers and armed vigilantes, with their white counterparts backing out, the Filipinos continued the strike and won their demands, including a 100 percent raise from twenty to forty cents an hour, improved working conditions, and recognition of the union. During the strike, Filipinos were often at odds with labor contractors—not just Chinese and Japanese but also Filipinos—who recruited Mexican, Punjabi, and Japanese strikebreakers. Despite conflicted origins, Filipino labor leaders such as Philip Vera Cruz and Larry Itliong would join with Mexican Americans—most famously Cesar Chavez—to better working conditions in the fields of California.

American-born generations introduced yet more variations in Asian ethnic identity formations. Although their citizenship and upbringing did not free them from racial restrictions and immersion in the enclaves, they nonetheless differed from the immigrant generation in their civic aspirations. Citizenship provided protections from deportation and the option of voting, significantly reframing possibilities for political participation. In 1895, Chinese Americans founded "Native Sons of the Golden State" for American-born generations; it eventually evolved into the Chinese American Citizens Alliance (CACA) when it became national in 1915. CACA advised Japanese Americans in founding the Japanese American Citizens League (JACL) in 1929. Both tended to attract the more educated, professional, and white-collar leadership members of their respective ethnic communities, while still sharing some major agendas with the immigrant generation. For example, the JACL joined with the JAA to challenge the 1922 Cable Act to regain citizenship status for US-born women, and supported the 1935 Nye-Lea bill to gain citizenship for World War I veterans.

Despite their status as citizens, US-born Asian Americans were excluded from school clubs and extracurricular activities, and so formed their own. Chinese Americans had their own ethnic-specific YWCAs and YMCAs, and service organizations such as the Square and Circle Club, Mei Wah Club, and Kuan Ying Girls Club. Southern California-based Korean Americans had clubs that held weekly dances and socials in the 1920s and 1930s. Japanese Americans displayed even higher levels of associational activities. In 1940, the *Rafu Shimpo* estimated there were four hundred youth organizations in southern California including high school girls' clubs, coed social service groups, women's athletic clubs, Japanese culture-study groups, dramatic and musical clubs, church-related youth leagues, the YWCA, the YMCA, the Young Men's Buddhist Association, and sorority and fraternity systems, with counterparts in major communities such as San Francisco, Seattle, and San Diego. For 1938, the newspaper reported only one day in the entire year (July 20) that Los Angeles lacked a *Nisei* club event. By the late 1930s, many rural areas had clubs as well, which were based in the local Japanese language and culture schools.

The depths of exclusion

Japanese Americans faced high levels of antagonism, despite and partially due to their very successes in demonstrating their capacities to attain key markers of good citizenship such as establishing multigenerational small family farms, organizing and dominating particular sectors of agricultural markets and distribution chains, and the compliance with American cultural norms, including high educational attainment and socialization of *Nisei*. Nonetheless, fears that Japanese would overrun agriculture in California and Washington state, both in establishing agricultural toeholds but also through children born with US citizenship, contributed to widely supported passage of the Alien Land Laws and pressures on the Japanese government to end the picture-bride practice in 1920. Over the objections of Japanese Americans, the Japanese government chose to mitigate tensions with the US government by cooperating.

World War II brought about the worst that Japanese Americans could have anticipated by sweeping away the communities they had created and claimed with such diligence and stubbornness on the West Coast. The rationale of "military necessity" targeted the essentialized foreignness of Japanese, even American-born citizens, in justifying their removal into "relocation camps" as "enemy aliens" identified by ancestry rather than place of birth and citizenship. This nadir of civil rights violations would, however, give rise to the conditional possibility for the integration of Asians into America.

For example, the Okubos, like many other Japanese American families, had eked out impressive levels of attainment despite sharply constricted circumstances. Mine Okubo (1912–2001) was one of seven children growing up in Riverside, California. Her mother was a calligrapher and her father a scholar who had arrived to study in 1904 and chose to stay in the United States. He could only find work in a candy factory and as a gardener while her mother raised the children. Nonetheless, Okubo managed to attend high school and Riverside Community College before transferring to the University of California at Berkeley, where she received her bachelor's and master's degrees and gained some prominence as an artist. When World War II broke out, Okubo was in Europe on a Bertha Taussig Memorial Traveling Fellowship. She returned to the United States and found a job with the Works Progress Administration in San Francisco, demonstrating the fresco technique of mural-making alongside the Mexican artist Diego Rivera.

In the early morning hours of December 7, 1941, Japanese planes struck Pearl Harbor and President Franklin D. Roosevelt signed Executive Order 9066 on February 19, 1942, authorizing the evacuation of Japanese and Japanese Americans on the West Coast. Issei leaders were swiftly rounded up, an 8 p.m. curfew was imposed, and bank accounts were frozen. Once it became clear that even citizen *Nisei* would be rounded up, about ten thousand Japanese moved voluntarily inland, outside the military zone, to avoid incarceration. The newlywed Kanemoto Hatsu and her husband moved from San Jose County to Colorado, where they found low-paying employment as farm laborers. Hatsu later deeply mourned their loss of autonomy and downgrade into a "hand-to-mouth" existence, as her family slid steadily into debt as sharecroppers farming onions and cabbages. Decades later she speculated that incarceration might have been a better option. Others such as Gordon Hirabayashi, Fred Korematsu, Yasui Minoru, and Endo Mitsuye challenged the curfew and evacuation orders as violations of their civil rights.

Over 120,000 Japanese Americans were removed from the West Coast, two-thirds of whom were US citizens. They were placed in ten "relocation centers" operated by the War Relocation Authority (WRA): Manzanar and Tule Lake, California; Poston and Gila River, Arizona; Topaz and Amache, Utah; Minidoka, Idaho; Heart Mountain, Wyoming; and Rohwer and Jerome, Arkansas.

Okubo was living in Berkeley when she received notification that she had three days to pack in preparation for a "pioneer life." She recorded her experiences through illustrations and long captions that appeared in *Citizen 13660* (1946), a text that captured both the dehumanizing eradication of her life as an American citizen, but also the resilience and humor that helped her survive.

She and a brother who was attending Berkeley were assigned to Tanforan, a converted racetrack in San Bruno where they resided temporarily in a twenty-by-nine-foot horse stall that still reeked of manure, and slept on beds made of rough sacks stuffed with hay. Bathroom facilities were hastily constructed trenches and everyone ate cafeteria-style, grateful despite the dismal food for the respite from boredom and complete uncertainty about the future. After six months, the Okubos were moved again, to the Topaz Relocation Center in Utah where, apart from the guards, Japanese Americans assumed almost complete responsibility for managing living necessities. Some drew upon their farming expertise to grow vegetables and grain to feed the camp, while others served as cooks, police, mess-hall attendants, construction workers, maintenance supervisors, teachers, and healthcare providers. They had lost their hard-won farms and homes and for the duration of the war had no choice but to make do amid the cold, windstorms, and dust that characterized most incarceration camps in crowded wooden barracks provisioned only with beds, stoves, and naked light bulbs. They did not know if and when they would be allowed to return to their homes or what might remain.

Kawahara Katsusaburo had to relinquish his painstakingly acquired holding of two hundred acres. He was forced to sell the crops and equipment below cost to a former schoolmate, while he turned over his farm to his Filipino employees to run in his absence. Japanese American misfortunes provided openings for other ethnic groups, as their now-profitable farms became available for whites and others to claim. For example, Filipino Toribio Castillo had struggled for over a decade as a migrant worker, busboy, and dishwasher to support his studies after arriving in 1928 as a student. Despite holding an MA degree from the University of Southern California, he only found employment as a domestic servant until the incarceration of Japanese Americans, when land became available for him to lease in Gardena. Less desirable niches also transferred with the departure of the Japanese. The journalist and social activist Carey McWilliams observed, "It was a foregone conclusion that Mexicans would be substituted as the major scapegoat group once the Japanese were removed" as the California press embarked on anti-Mexican campaigns criticizing juvenile delinquency and gang activity in the early 1940s.

Other Asian Americans, particularly Chinese and Filipinos, had their own reasons to be unsympathetic to the incarceration of Japanese Americans. Japan's invasions of their homelands and the ensuing brutal conditions there, along with economic competition in the United States, produced generally mixed responses. As hostile Anglos often did not distinguish between Asian "enemies" or "friends," those remaining on the West Coast faced anti-Japanese hostilities, with some beaten up, even during the day. Or, their cars were wrecked or overturned and their tires slashed, leading some to use identifying pins and signs declaring "We hate the Japs worse than you do."

The globe-spanning alliances and enmities of international war intensified, but then ultimately unraveled, the essentialized foreignness of Asian Americans. The race-based imprisonment of all West-Coast Japanese crystallized long-standing legal definitions of Asians as "aliens ineligible for citizenship," applying even to US-born generations. From the beginning, however, incarceration was shot through with contradictions. Hawaiian Japanese were not rounded up to avoid the collapse of the local economy; within months of being placed in "relocation centers" select Japanese were released away from the West Coast for agricultural labor, military service, study, and employment; and the centers claimed to operate both as protection for Japanese and to preclude them from espionage. Amid this storm of conflicting messages regarding the civil rights of Japanese Americans, their questioned national loyalties, and the exigencies of "military necessity," the head of the JACL, Mike Masaoka, emerged as a controversial but key leader urging Japanese Americans to display compliance and martial patriotism despite the violations of incarceration. In 1941, Masaoka had authored the JACL creed which stated, despite historical experience to the contrary:

> Although some individuals may discriminate against me, I shall never become bitter or lose faith, for I know that such persons are not representative of the majority of the American people. True, I shall do all in my power to discourage such practices, but I shall do it in the American way—above board, in the open, through courts of law, by education, by proving myself to be worthy of equal treatment and consideration. I am firm in my belief that American sportsmanship and attitude of fair play will judge citizenship and patriotism on the basis of action and achievement, and not on the basis of physical characteristics.

An early volunteer for military service, Masaoka urged fellow Japanese Americans to establish records of good citizenship, and fully embrace American national prerogatives and patriotism, in order to pave a pathway for Japanese and other Asians out of this murky swamp of intentions, categorizations, and institutional practices, and to help them gain status as exemplary Americans—a transformation quickly accomplished in the years after World War II.

Chapter 4
Crucibles of war

The remaking of Japanese into model American citizens began during their worst crisis of exclusion. Despite the sweeping urgency of "military necessity," which was used to justify the incarceration of all West Coast Japanese Americans, a significant minority, including *Nisei* such as Mine Okubo (1912–2001), were released well before the end of World War II. In January 1944, Okubo made her way to New York when *Fortune* magazine offered her a job as an illustrator.

The terms of her departure required that she complete the 1943 Loyalty Registration, in which imprisoned Japanese Americans were asked to declare their support for the United States, rather than Japan, and citizens were required to affirm their willingness to serve in the American armed forces. In this way, five out of every six Japanese Americans formally pledged their American loyalty, thereby clearing the way for their release; the noncompliant minority, on the other hand, were punished, some by being sent to Tule Lake with the label "no-no boys," because they had refused to affirm loyalty to the United States. Despite such significant levels of dissent, Japanese Americans survived the deep setbacks of ·incarceration to embark on a path that, within two decades, positioned them as model US patriots unquestionably deserving of the full rights of citizens. As would other Asian Americans, Japanese emerged from the forges of World War II and the Cold War, which burnt away the surface attributions of racial stigma in purifying their incontrovertible claims to full status as Americans on the basis of shared political and economic values.

Okubo's contribution to this recuperation stemmed from her detailed record of daily life in the camps, evoked through closely observed charcoal, watercolor, and pen-and-ink sketches. The resulting series produced a deeply humane, often humorous account of the deprivations of camp life, marked by housing in hastily converted horse stables and recently erected military barracks; the long queues for basic necessities such as latrines; and cafeteria-style meals, showers, and postal services; all with scant opportunities for privacy or individuality. Okubo's images revealed the resilient reconstruction of some semblance of normality through the planting of gardens; the organizing of schools, newspapers, and adult classes; and the running of services needed for entirely new communities ranging upwards of ten thousand people. Published with succinctly evocative text in 1946, *Citizen 13660* gently depicted the stripping away of Japanese American rights, even as it underscored their compliance and dignity in enduring great suffering—a portrayal that vindicated efforts to permit and advance Japanese American integration.

The exemplary patriotism of Japanese Americans gained even greater resonance through the heroism of the combined 442nd Regimental Combat Team, which absorbed the 100th Infantry Battalion to lay down a still unmatched record of bravery and sacrifice. The most decorated unit of its size in US history, the segregated 442nd drew upon 3,600 recruited from the camps and about 22,000 others who lived in Hawaii or outside the relocation zone for some of the riskiest missions in Europe. Those *Nisei* with sufficient Japanese-language skills, often *kibei* or *Nisei* who had studied in Japan and who had been considered the greatest loyalty risks, worked in intelligence as interpreters and translators. The 442nd's valor and national service, etched in blood and death, crowned the cooperation of noncombatant Japanese Americans with US "military necessity," providing potent fodder for the JACL,

7. **Japanese American artist Mine Okubo regularly inserted herself as an observer in her drawings of incarceration. In this drawing, she stands in the left foreground with a windswept forelock wearing a patterned shirt as testament to the lines that were a daily trial of life in incarceration camps.**

which was working with various branches of the US government to validate the claims of Japanese to full inclusion in the United States. JACL leader Mike Masaoka consulted for the 1951 Hollywood film *Go for Broke!*, which celebrated these newly proclaimed American heroes. However, this redemptive process required omission of those Japanese who had rejected or only reluctantly embraced American patriotism and mainstream values, such as those 5,589 *Nisei* who had renounced their US citizenship, the no-no boys who had refused to serve in the military, or the zoot-suited rowdies known as "*pachuke.*" Asian integration emerged on terms that affirmed expanding powers for the federal government, as well as economic competitiveness agendas.

Recuperation of Japanese American rights and status proceeded even as judicial review of incarceration affirmed federal powers to target racialized groups in cases of "military necessity" at the expense of individual civil rights. The JACL chose Endo Mitsuye as a test case because she was an Americanized *Nisei* who was a practicing Christian, had never been to Japan, spoke only English, and had a brother in the US Army. The writ of habeas corpus challenging her detention as a US citizen worked its way through the judicial system slowly, so that not until December 18, 1944 did the Supreme Court issue a decision ruling unanimously in *Ex parte Mitsuye Endo* (323 U.S. 283), finding that the War Relocation Authority (WRA) did not have the authority to detain a citizen whom the US government found to be "concededly loyal." This ruling paved the way for mass releases without challenging the basic premise of "military necessity" when undertaken by the federal government. The same day, the Supreme Court ruled 6–3, in the case of *Korematsu v. United States* (323 U.S. 214), that the exclusion order was constitutional and affirmed the federal government's authority in times of "military necessity" to act against members of a minority group whose ancestral homeland nation was at war with the United States.

This principle also applied to the cases of Gordon Hirabayashi and Yasui Minoru, who had both deliberately violated the curfew imposed on Japanese Americans to produce court challenges, but lost. "Military necessity" survived as a justification for the violation of civil rights even when the convictions of Korematsu, Hirabayashi, and Yasui were vacated during the 1980s, when it came to light that evidence had been suppressed showing that the Naval Office had investigated and found no evidence of Japanese American espionage. "Military necessity" remains an active governing principle in the early twenty-first century and sanctions federal actions, such as the ongoing US operation of prison facilities at Guantanamo Bay.

s quickly as incarceration began, the federal government wound own its wholesale uprooting of West Coast Japanese Americans.

Forewarned of the Supreme Court's decisions, the White House had rescinded the exclusion orders a day earlier to declare that Japanese Americans could begin returning to the West Coast, starting in January 1945. The porousness of "military necessity" had been revealed as early as 1942, when the WRA released some Japanese for agricultural work in areas outside the sensitive West Coast. Starting March 1942 and running through 1946, the WRA worked with the National Japanese American Student Relocation Council in assisting 3,613 students to enroll in 680 colleges and universities, mostly in the Rocky Mountain and Midwest regions.

The bulk of Japanese American citizens of "conceded" loyalty began returning to the West Coast early in 1945, although the last camp did not close until March 1946. Despite WRA efforts to assist, returning, resettling, and starting over was hard. Katie Hironaka was in her mid-twenties when she left Heart Mountain with her parents to return to San Jose. Her parents initially had to stay at a Buddhist temple that had been converted into a hostel while Katie sheltered with her in-laws in a barn until they could regain footing. Many older issei without younger relatives could not re-establish their lives and ended up in county institutions. A visible minority never returned to the West Coast and remade their lives in the Midwest or the East, where they had been forcibly resettled.

Hostilities lingered in the immediate aftermath of the war, such as outbreaks of arson. Sakauye Eiichi recalled receiving a placard in his mailbox saying "Send All Japs back to Japan." Nonetheless he managed to stay on his family's farm, growing pears, celery, and bell peppers; he remained an active farmer in San Jose into the 1990s. Limited employment opportunities, however, led most Japanese Americans to seek alternatives, as the back of their enclave economy had been broken. In Santa Clara County, Japanese Americans fared somewhat better than elsewhere because they helped with labor shortages in the area; Kanemoto Hatsu recalled that many became berry sharecroppers who did not really compete with whites specializing in orchard fruits. Other Japanese moved into new endeavors—grocery stores, domestic service, gardening for hire, or other employment using their agricultural expertise—while growing numbers of *Nisei* and third-generation *Sansei* with college educations were able to enter white-collar and professional fields. Alongside Asians from World War II allies, Japanese also benefited from the veterans' benefits ensuing from military service and the diminishing of discrimination in housing, education, and employment. Access to such markers of middle-class success fostered the image that America's multiracial democracy was enabling Japanese Americans, so recently incarcerated as enemy aliens, to attain upward social mobility, thus serving as a powerful vindication that the United States was shedding its ugly segregationist past.

The rapid onset of the Cold War dramatically improved the standing of Japanese Americans, as China turned communist (1949) and the Korean War (1950–1952) split the peninsula, thereby transforming Japan into America's chief ally in the western Pacific. The firm American hand of General Douglas MacArthur molded the occupation and restitution of Japan's constitution and modern economic and political institutions. Domestically, impressions of Japanese Americans improved as they entered a greater range of occupations and their ethnic enclaves, both urban and rural, were dismantled through incarceration. Some social scientists interpreted this coerced form of dispersal as positive indicators that Japanese Americans were finally integrating. The lobbyist Mike Masaoka promoted the sacrifices of the 442nd and compliance at camp to press Congress into legislating more equitable rights for Japanese as Americans. Such civil rights advocacy quickly started paying off, with the 1947 amendment to the War Brides Act allowing an exception so that even Japanese "aliens ineligible for citizenship" married or engaged to military veterans could immigrate, and the 1948 Evacuation Claims Act that brought some measures of financial compensation for incarceration. Exclusionary barriers fell even earlier on behalf of Asian Americans whose homeland states had been American allies during World War II. The conditions and options for Asian integration continued to evolve and expand along with the reworking of domestic racial ideologies and immigration priorities that accompanied US efforts to claim leadership of the free world during the ensuing Cold War.

The crumbling walls of Asian exclusion

War waged on a global stage elevated the importance of international alliances as well as enmities in framing access to immigration and citizenship for Asians, with longer-term consequences for the shedding of racist nationalisms, segregation, and collaborations based on shared political and economic values. The worldwide struggle against communism compelled the United States to cultivate friendships with Asian nations and peoples, including the many emergent postcolonial states such as India, Korea, Vietnam, Taiwan, Malaysia, Cambodia, Indonesia, and Burma. The walls of Asian exclusion crumbled with the piecemeal abolishing of laws restricting immigration, citizenship, employment, residence, and miscegenation, underwritten by a reworking of racial ideologies and immigration controls that remade Asians into model immigrants and citizens, even as it positioned them as innately suited for educational attainment and economic success.

The dismantling of exclusion began with a reconsideration of the status of Chinese, as the United States' chief World War II ally against Japan. Japanese propaganda citing the exclusion laws as a reason for Chinese to abandon the United States and ally with Japan on the basis of race pushed Congress to swiftly enact repeal in 1943. The door opened with a three-month national speaking tour by Madame Chiang Kai-shek, the Methodist, US-educated, fashionable wife of China's leader, including enthusiastically received talks before both houses of Congress and at Madison Square Garden, and a lavish, Hollywood-style production before twenty thousand at the Hollywood Bowl. Formerly Soong Mei-ling (and still one of Wellesley College's most famous alumni), Madame Chiang demonstrated with intelligence and charm how well-educated Chinese could display core US values of democracy, independence, and Christianity. Congressman Walter Judd, a former medical missionary in China and outspoken advocate for improving US ties in East Asia, forcefully argued for repeal by observing that under the 1924 Immigration Act, Adolf Hitler could immigrate and naturalize, but Madame Chiang could not. More pragmatically, Judd made repeal more palatable by reminding restrictionist legislators that if Chinese were admitted through the same national origins quota system as Europeans, even if they received naturalization rights, they could only enter at a rate of 105 per year, thereby ensuring minimal impact. In practical terms, repeal produced few improvements in the daily lives of Chinese Americans, although acknowledging the principle that they merited equal consideration for immigration and citizenship was a significant symbolic advance.

Once cracked open, America's gate swung wider to admit token numbers of other Asian groups as well. Indians and Filipinos were next, with the 1946 Luce-Celler Act. Filipinos at last gained the independence promised with the Tydings-McDuffie Act, as well as naturalization rights along with a tiny immigration quota, as did Indians. Dalip Singh Saund quickly took advantage of the change in laws to claim his long-awaited citizenship and then run for office, becoming the first Asian American elected to national office in 1956, when he won the House seat for Congressional District 29. Saund had arrived as a student in 1919 and received a PhD in mathematics but worked as a farmer under the restrictions of exclusion. Nonetheless he avidly participated in local party politics, developing a long resume of civic activism that quickly launched his political career once he became eligible. Racial segregation quickly dissipated in other arenas as well. Military service transformed Chinese and Filipinos into veterans who had earned certain benefits, such as naturalization, the right to bring spouses and fiancées into the country, education, and access to a broader array of employment through training they had received. During the late 1940s, courts began casting out discriminatory laws such as the alien land acts, anti-miscegenation statutes, and residential housing covenants.

As former enemy aliens, Japanese were the last Asian group to break through the legal markers of Asian exclusion to gain naturalization rights and immigration quotas. For these reasons, the JACL supported the 1952 McCarran-Walter Act, which abolished altogether the racial bar on citizenship and granted immigration quotas to all nations along with other small measures of reform: first preference for employment categories; non-quota immigration rights for close family members of US citizens; and parole authority for the attorney general to admit refugees in cases of emergencies. Nonetheless, many reform groups sharply criticized the law for retaining the discriminatory national-origins quotas and for continuing the racial tracking of Asians, and Asians alone, through the Asian-Pacific Triangle, which capped entries at two thousand per year. For such reasons, President Harry Truman vetoed the law, only to have his veto overturned by Congress.

Despite these flaws, the McCarran-Walter Act enacted a preference system that enabled a more flexible process for selective admissions that could further economic and political priorities and de-emphasize problematical considerations of race and national origins. The trade-offs and competing options gained focus through the quandary of twelve thousand elite Chinese who became refugees when World War II, the Chinese Civil War (1946–1949), and the Communist victory blocked their return home. The so-called "stranded students" were largely well-educated and networked, and their ranks included highly elite postgraduate students, talented and experienced technical and economic trainees, academic and cultural exchange representatives, Nationalist diplomats and officials, and wealthy tourists. Should such useful, strategically potent individuals be forced to leave the United States and become communist simply because short-sighted laws constrained their immigration rights based on their race? With the future employment of exceptionally talented Chinese such as the architect I. M. Pei, the computer entrepreneur An Wang, and the 1957 Nobel Prize-winning physicists T. D. Lee and C. N. Yang at stake, Congress took the unprecedented step of allocating $10 million and passing laws to enable the "stranded" to remain and complete their academic programs (many to the level of PhDs) and find legal employment—only to run afoul of quota limits when seeking permanent status to remain.

Limited refugee measures, such as the 1948 Displaced Persons Act and the 1953 Refugee Relief Act, reveal most clearly the political pressures leading the United States to express its sympathy and support for fellow anti-communist peoples by providing them safe haven and new homes. American concern for Europeans in crisis was much greater—as conveyed through the amount of resources and refugee visas allocated—but the conferral of even symbolic gestures of sympathy for Asians reflected significant shifts. In the 1953 Act, Asians received only 5,000 of the 214,000 refugee visas made available. After this program ended in 1956, Congress voted to reallocate the many unused European visas from this program to oversubscribed areas, such as the Far and Middle East. Although the 1960 Refugee Act sponsored by Francis Walter continued to privilege Europeans and exclude Asians by definition, arousing great protest, in 1962, just over 15,000 Chinese refugees were paroled into the United States with comfortable levels of political and popular support.

As it became clear that the People's Republic of China (PRC) was stabilizing during the 1950s, and that Chinese refugees resident in the United States would not be able to return to an allied China, their long-term prospects applied pressures for immigration reforms that advanced economic and political priorities by emphasizing shared values as well as individual skills and qualifications. Additional urgency accrued from PRC invitations to overseas Chinese scientists to return and rebuild the motherland. The mishandled defection of Caltech-based rocket scientist Qian Xuesen in 1955, and the Soviet launching of Sputnik in October 1957, both underscored the dire competition for the most valuable of scientific and technical talent for purposes of research and development, regardless of racial and national origin. Special programs allowed Pei and Wang to naturalize in 1955 and secure their futures in the United States, but the general problem of the restrictive permanent immigration law remained. After World War II, steady influxes of students from China, India, Japan, and South Korea readily found jobs legally in the United States, particularly in technical, white-collar, and professional fields during the 1950s and 1960s, but they ran into severe problems when trying to convert to permanent status. Their evident utility to US economic development came to displace the far less palatable image of manual laborers, service workers, ethnic slums and bachelor communities, and cheap restaurants once associated with Asian Americans—a shift that compelled rethinking of the immigration laws designed to keep low their immigrant numbers.

By 1940, Asian exclusion had clearly worked, in part through the institutionalization of border controls and also because geography severely, although never completely, constricted the capacity of Asians to enter in defiance of US laws, and the Great Depression diminished motivations to migrate. During the 1930s, only 4,928 Chinese had immigrated, along with 1,948 Japanese and Koreans, 781 Filipinos (since 1934), and 496 Indians, in stark contrast to the hundreds of thousands of Mexicans crossing the shared southern border each year. Even the symbolic unravelling of Asian exclusion beginning in the 1940s maintained extremely low levels of Asian admissions: just under 25,000 for these five main groups during that decade. The high degree of enforceability of immigration laws against Asians fostered the realization, compounded by economic and political exigencies of the Cold War, that border controls could be used not only as defensive measures keeping out unwelcome threats, but also as screening mechanisms encouraging the migration of individuals identified as advantageous to the United States.

Politics, particularly anti-communism, assumed perhaps paramount importance in the context of the Cold War, presenting both crisis and opportunity for Asian Americans. Military patriotism during World War II and the US occupation of Japan afterwards set Japanese Americans on the path toward full recuperation by 1952. Chinese abruptly became the greatest potential villains of Asia. The ascendance of Mao Zedong and the PRC, and the outbreak of the Korean War, positioned Chinese Americans as potential security risks, with the 1950 McCarran Internal Security Act sounding echoes of incarceration in authorizing emergency detention for those thought likely to engage in espionage or sabotage. The controversial "loss of China" by America's long-cultivated allies of the Nationalists and Chiang Kai-shek inspired Joseph McCarthy's earliest witch hunts for communist conspirators and remained a smoking gun wielded by the China Lobby—an influential coterie of Nationalist supporters including old China hands, businessmen, missionaries, politicians, and Nationalist representatives—to block the PRC's admission into the United Nations until 1971. Long-standing practices of immigration through fraudulent statuses—the so-called "paper son" system—raised alarms as a possible means of entry for communist spies, as did efforts by the communist government to demand remittances from Chinese overseas for their relatives in China. Mainstream Chinese Americans put on overt displays of anti-communism by flying Nationalist flags and embracing American values of capitalism and democracy, by pursuing the expanding array of economic opportunities opening up to them and becoming more civically active.

As it had with the agonizing Loyalty Registration of Japanese Americans in camp, the federal government implemented another highly divisive program, intended in the case of Chinese to eliminate "paper-son slots" to prevent entry by spies, use fraudulent entry status to prosecute suspected communists and leftist sympathizers, and then to regularize the status of democratically aligned resident Chinese so that they could be more fully integrated. Decades of failure to systematically identify Chinese fraudulent identities, despite extensive documentary and testamentary requirements and investigative measures, led the FBI and INS to develop the Confession Program (1956–1965) to induce Chinese Americans to voluntarily reveal their entire real and paper-son lineages in exchange for regularized status and use of their real names. After decades of mistreatment by immigration authorities, only about a quarter of Chinese Americans took part, and most did so unwillingly, implicated in the confessions of others. Despite low rates of participation, the Confession Program was declared a success and ended with the passage of the 1965 Hart-Celler Act's family reunification provisions, which were believed to render immigration fraud unnecessary for Chinese.

The sanctioning, and even welcoming, of Asian presences in the United States evolved on other fronts. After World War II, Congress and the State Department expanded soft diplomatic programs intended to advance US influence overseas through educational, technical, and cultural exchanges, as symbolized most visibly by the Fulbright (1947) and Smith-Mundt (1948) Acts. Seen as cheap alternatives to military deployments, exchange programs could influence the educated elites and other potential leaders through person-to-person contacts involving travel, temporary residency, and exposure to cultural, economic, and bureaucratic institutions and values, particularly in the cases of developing nations. The opportunity to shape nations, so aborted in the case of China, flourished with the dozens of decolonization efforts resulting from World War II. Koreans joyously declared their independence with Japan's defeat on August 15, 1945 and in 1948 elected the first president of the Republic of Korea, Synghman Rhee, who had spent years in the United States studying and then lobbying for independence. The Philippines gained nationhood from American colonization on July 4, 1946 and Pakistan and India gained independence from Britain on August 14 and 15, respectively, in 1947. Over the next several decades, the nations of Malaysia, Indonesia, Vietnam, Burma, Bangladesh, Cambodia, Laos, and dozens of others emerged from colonization in Asia as well. Brought together in the global forum of the United Nations, which was established on October 24, 1945, these Asians nations and their peoples attained a marker of equal standing with the United States that required acknowledgment of their sovereignty and foreign interests. One strategy was to send successful Asian Americans on speaking tours of Asia to personally convey the benevolence of American democracy. This program had varying degrees of success through representatives such as medical doctor, Olympic gold medal-winning diver, and military veteran Sammy Lee (b. 1920), author and ceramicist Jade Snow Wong (1922–2006), painter Dong Kingman (1911–2000), and the aforementioned Representative Saund.

In this changing landscape of international relations, and compelled by the Cold War to foster friendships around the world, people-to-people cultural exchanges and international education programs constituted relatively inexpensive and easily publicized systems to cultivate connections and influence abroad, while seeking to inculcate compatible political and economic values and institutions. The success of such collaborations had been demonstrated in earlier programs to bring students and future leaders from Asia to study in the United States, through international education projects such as the *pensionado* program in the Philippines, the Boxer Indemnity Fellowships, and the Chinese Educational Mission. After World War II, the numbers of international students coming to the United States increased from 10,341 in 1945–1946, to 29,813 in 1950–1951, eventually reaching 764,495 in 2011–2012, with students from Asian countries such as India, South Korea, Taiwan, Japan, and, after 1979, China often included in the ten most numerous international student populations.

Under the guise of international education and exchange, such programs often furthered explicitly political US aims abroad. For example, the Michigan State University Vietnam Advisory Group program (MSUVAG), which ran from 1955 until 1962, reflects the Cold War intersections between US anti-communist engagements overseas, international exchange programs, and Asian immigration. The US Department of State funded this program to extend technical assistance under the management of faculty and staff from Michigan State University (MSU), particularly political science professor Wesley Fishel, a personal friend of the Republic of Vietnam (RVN) president Ngô Đình Diệm, and MSU president John Hannah, a friend of President Eisenhower and a staunch anti-communist.

MSUVAG was part of Hannah's vision for promoting applied knowledge, which in the case of Vietnam included helping to write its new constitution; posting MSU faculty to advise and train Vietnamese regarding rural economic development and administrative training of bureaucratic personnel and political leaders; and training consultation and arming of police and security forces. MSUVAG's Participant Program brought 179 Vietnamese to study at MSU in fields such as public administration, political science, economics, finance, and police administration, alongside observation of operations in relevant government agencies. This carefully selected elite earned higher degrees, often doctorates in fields such as public administration and economics, and returned to teach and train other Vietnamese in the institutional strategies and culture of the United States. As the United States' massive investment in bolstering a noncommunist government in Vietnam failed dismally, many of these MSUVAG-trained professionals and bureaucrats were among the first waves of refugees paroled into the United States starting in 1975, as those with the closest, and therefore most damning, ties to the United States, which also made them more welcome and assimilable in the land of their training.

This dynamic operated more broadly across the post-World War II era, as international education and exchange programs intended to train Asian elites to extend US influence in their homelands simultaneously produced educated and readily employable and acculturated Asians who were highly compatible candidates for immigration. Growing numbers from allied states such as Taiwan, South Korea, India, and Hong Kong, attended US institutions of higher education, often specializing in science, technology, engineering, and math (STEM) fields, which facilitated legal employment after graduation and the option that employers could apply for their conversion to legal residency under the terms of the 1952 McCarran-Walter Act. Although the severely limited quota allocations placed such "first preference" applicants onto extremely long waiting lists, with quota slots for Chinese mortgaged through the year 2036 by 1957, administrative practices such as deferrals of deportation, occasional opportunities for legal adjustments, marriage to citizens, and private Congressional bills enabled many to remain despite experiences of extended legal limbos. For example, the Exchange Visitor Program (EVP), a "temporary" training program first established in 1948, resulted in permanent resettlement of about eleven thousand Filipina nurses arriving to work in the United States between 1956 and 1968, often through marriage or with the assistance of the hospitals in which they worked.

The migration of such educated, skilled workers, particularly those in technology fields required for research and development, had become priorities for economic and military competitiveness during the Cold War. The multifaceted conflict between the United States and the Soviet Union pitted capitalist against communist economic and political systems and generated an urgency revealed perhaps most intensely in the nuclear arms and space races. The launching of the Soviet Sputnik space capsule in October 1957, hydrogen bomb testing, and the Cuban missile crisis underscored the vital importance of cultivating and retaining the world's best scientific and technical talents, depending upon their political values and regardless of their racial ancestry.

Despite the urgency of this cause, the complexities of Congressional legislative processes delayed immigration reforms even though Presidents Truman, Eisenhower, and Kennedy all pressed for immigration laws to shed their overt racial preferences—applied to Asians through the Asian-Pacific Triangle and unequal quotas—to better serve international relations purposes and advance US economic agendas. Stopgap measures addressed but failed to permanently resolve the problem.

For example, in 1957, after the 1953 Refugee Relief program ended without dispensing all its visas, particularly in Europe, Congress authorized redistribution to oversubscribed areas, such as the Far East, prioritizing the degree of professional, technical, or other skills and reunification of families. This law also gave the attorney general power to relieve oversubscribed quotas by adjusting the statuses of a "limited number" of skilled aliens present on July 1, 1957 who possessed approved first-preference petitions filed before September 11, 1957. Extending this preference for skilled workers, in 1962, Public Law 87-885 removed quota restrictions on the thousands of first-preference applicants waiting in line for permanent residency, thus opening the United States' gates to the influxes of engineers, medical personnel, scientists, and other educated, professional, and white-collar workers that would come to be known by 1966 as "brain drain," after passage of the 1965 Immigration Act that permanently enacted these priorities. In the two decades prior, however, US state policy, international relations agencies, and economic departments had already been reworking conditions of migration and immigration to the United States that would produce Asian immigrants as model minority subjects: educated, employable, hard-working, and politically compliant.

Attaining the mainstream

Mainstream media productions such as books, plays, musicals, and movies celebrated US outreach in Asia and the domestication of its Asian population along with consumption of Asian cultures. Buwei Yang Chao's *How to Cook and Eat in Chinese* (1945) was reprinted in three editions and was the first popular, English-language guide to cooking Chinese food; it spurred American housewives to produce Chinese food in their own kitchens using American ingredients. Jade Snow Wong's memoir, *Fifth Chinese Daughter* (1950) paralleled Monica Sone's *Nisei Daughter* (1953) in airing the struggles of young women to claim their own voices and individuality despite growing up in patriarchal families. The film *Back to Bataan* (1945) conveyed crucial Filipino support for US war efforts in the Pacific, as *Go for Broke!* did for the 442nd. Other films, such as *Teahouse of the August Moon* (1956) and *The King and I* (1956), depicted comic miscommunication between Westerners serving as advisors posted to Asian societies, but emphasized American benevolent interest. The "stranded student" author C. Y. Lee published *Flower Drum Song* (1957), which became the basis for Rodgers and Hammerstein's highly successful Broadway musical of the same name in 1958, which in turn generated the popular screen adaptation of 1961 memorably showcasing Nancy Kwan, Miyoshi Umeki, and the songs "Chop Suey" and "Grant Avenue, USA," all celebrating Chinese versions of American life.

No less than three Rodgers and Hammerstein musicals featured themes concerning the coming together of Western and Asian characters and cultures: the Tony-award-winning *The King and I* (1946), *Flower Drum Song*, and *South Pacific* (1949), based upon the Pulitzer-Prize winning book by James Michener, *Tales of the South Pacific* (1947). *South Pacific* not only featured a multicultural cast and exotic setting, it also urged acceptance of miscegenation, with the main character, nurse Nellie Forbush, having to learn to accept her French suitor's half-Polynesian children.

Michener, who married a Japanese American woman in 1955, authored several bestselling books featuring Americans in Asia and the Pacific such as *Hawaii* (1959), *The Bridges at Toko-ri* (1953), and the semiautobiographical *Sayonara* (1954). The last was made into a 1957 movie starring Marlon Brando that advocated for romances and marriages between white military officers and Japanese women in occupied Japan, and featured Umeki in the role that made her the first Asian American actor to win an Academy Award, in 1958. Reportedly, Brando filmed *Sayonara* in atonement for his yellow-face turn as a biracial interpreter in *Teahouse of the August Moon*, which was based upon the Pulitzer-Prize-winning play (1953) by John Patrick, who had also written the screenplay for the 1960 movie *World of Suzie Wong*, drawing on the 1957 novel by Richard Mason and again starring the biracial Nancy Kwan, who played a Hong Kong prostitute redeemed through her relationship with a poor American painter. Across the 1950s, art and life intersected with the integration and racial mixing of Asians into American culture, where they emerged as increasingly naturalized aspects of culture and society.

When amending the War Brides Act in 1947 to admit "aliens ineligible for citizenship"—by then a category applying primarily to Japanese and Koreans—Congress understood that in doing so it was sanctioning mixed-race marriages. Although *Nisei* were the primary intended beneficiaries, legislators acknowledged that white and black military personnel had also formed relationships with Asians and that some would seek to bring these spouses and fiancées to the United States. In those early years of the policy, military administrators imposed procedural blocks to discourage mixed-race marriages, as depicted in *Sayonara*, but in the decades since, military marriages of primarily Asian women to American men have been a major route of entry into the United States and have resulted in the highest levels of out-marriage in populations hosting American military bases such as Japanese, Koreans, Filipinos, and Vietnamese. Rest and recreation sites in Hong Kong and Thailand also produced tourism and interracial sex.

Military deployments fostered other forms of intimacy that produced new immigration flows which placed Asians into mixed-race American families. War, occupation, and the long-term presence of military bases perhaps inevitably produced children, mixed-race and sometimes outcast, who became ready subjects for American succor. Since the 1930s, needy Asian children, subsisting under conditions of war and destitution, were among the most compelling targets for American sympathy and aid, ranging from token G.I. gifts of candy and gum, and charitable institutions such as schools, orphanages, and hospitals, to permanent adoption into American families. The relatively innocent engagements between American adults and Asian children mitigated the seamier reality that the wealth and advantages privileging US military bases and associated personnel fostered attending services in the form of nightlife and prostitution. The entrenchment of US military presence in Asia through World War II, the occupation of Japan, the Korean War, bases in the Philippines, Thailand, Taiwan, and Okinawa, and the Vietnam War, brought Americans into steady contact with impoverished, orphaned, or cast-off biracial children who became causes célèbres, with outspoken advocates such as Pearl Buck and the evangelists Harry and Bertha Holt, the latter of whom founded agencies facilitating inter-country, transracial adoptions that quickly gained popularity and general acceptance. The American urge to rescue needy Asian children built upon longstanding missionary projects, which had been sundered from their major investments in China by the Cold War.

The proliferation of Asians as members of mixed-race families signaled the dissipating racialization of Asians as essentially different and foreign even as the presumption by many adoptive parents, often white, evangelical Christians residing in the Midwest, that Asian ancestry would not affect their children's lives produced varying degrees of trauma and dislocation. Initially, refugee legislation provided the legal grounds for such immigration, starting with the Displaced Persons Act of 1948, and continued through the piecemeal, limited-term refugee laws of the 1950s. So powerfully did these adoptions work upon the imaginations and desires of aspiring, American adoptive parents, however, that this newly powerful constituency sought to make permanent their access to needy Asian children by persuading Congress to legislatively transform inter-country adoptees from refugees into family members for immigration purposes in an Act of September 26, 1961. In conjunction with refugee admissions and the facilitated immigration of first-preference workers, the walls of Asian exclusion were breaking down so that Asian Americans could claim access and statuses more proximate to that of the most favored immigrant streams.

These minor shifts in immigration laws began significantly remaking the demographic profile of Asian Americans even before the transformative impact of the 1965 Immigration Act, in part because such high percentages are foreign-born. Leaving behind their pasts as male-dominated, marginalized communities made up of migratory workers, Asian American communities diversified in ways that have since enabled the attribution of model minority status that now predominates in the early twenty-first century: educational attainment; professional and white-collar employment; over-representation in science and technology fields; suburban residence; and a general feminization and infantilization, in the sense that they were perceived as relatively weak and nonthreatening.

Many post-World War II newcomers arrived as outsiders to established ethnic communities for various reasons. Although many immigrated through family reunification provisions of the McCarran-Walter Act and refugee laws, thousands of refugees and first-preference immigrants entered without connections to traditional ethnic enclaves. These trends have perhaps been most visible among Koreans, with the majority of those entering from 1951 until 1964 doing so as war brides, adopted children, and students. From 1959 until 1965, 70 percent of Koreans arriving as immigrants were women with the status of military spouses.

Mixed in with these largely unskilled workers were 6 percent arriving as professionals and managers, indicating that even before 1965, employment considerations were starting to shape the Korean American population. Through the infusion of these new kinds of immigrants, the tiny population of about 7,500 Koreans in 1950 multiplied five-fold to about 45,000 in 1965.

From 1940 to 1960, the Chinese American population more than doubled, from 106,334 to 237,292, in large part through family reunification, as women and children joined men in the United States. For the first time, more women than men immigrated, enabling greater numbers of families so that by 1965, about 55 percent of Chinese Americans were American-born. However, perhaps the most visible of Chinese Americans during these years were immigrants arriving with technical, scientific and professional skills—such as the computer entrepreneur An Wang of Wang Computers—who reached previously inaccessible levels of success and integration as intellectuals finding employment in universities and colleges, even as many urban Chinese remained mired in the more limited ethnic-enclave employment of small businesses, restaurants, and textile manufacturing. In conjunction with growing numbers of American-born entering technical and professional fields, these new immigrants contributed to the segmented representation of Chinese Americans in the labor market characterizing the early twenty-first century.

South Asians started exhibiting this bifurcation as well. A small group before World War II, South Asians continued to immigrate in low numbers before 1965, with the population increasing from only 2,405 in 1940 to about 12,296 in 1960, largely through the arrivals of students and intellectuals seeking higher education and then employment.

The shifts in immigration law brought greater gender balance to the largely male Filipino American community in several ways. Service in the US military during World War II conferred the opportunity for naturalization, which several thousand Filipinos undertook annually through the 1940s and 1950s, thereby gaining the ability to bring over wives and children. Through these processes, and by "brain drain," by 1965, the numbers of adult Filipino men and women had reached parity. Despite relatively modest immigration numbers, the community grew through natural increase from 122,707 in 1950 to 176,310 in 1960. Among the relatively low numbers of immigrants, increasing percentages arrived as professionals, growing from 9.2 percent in 1959 to 18.1 percent in 1963.

Japanese also immigrated chiefly through family reunification and in greater numbers than any other Asian nationalities between 1952 and 1965. For example, 84,000 Japanese foreign spouses immigrated from 1945 until 1985, constituting over half of the total immigration of 154,000 Japanese. Apart from those who married *Nisei*, most were situated in the United States through the families and communities of white or black military spouses. Japanese remained the largest Asian American population from 1910 until 1970, after which immigration by other Asian nationalities overtook them in numbers. Although most of these new immigrants, or *shin issei*, arrived without professional or technical backgrounds, the Japanese American community's overall educational and employment profiles improved through the attainments of US-born *Nisei* and the next generation *Sansei*. Their greater orientation and access to American society provided the skills and motivation to demand even greater integration into the mainstream, even as ideological and immigration shifts were in the process of transforming Asians into a supra-accomplished group that would demonstrate the elimination of racial differentiation altogether.

Struggles for inclusion

Asian American claims for greater political and cultural inclusion expanded with the ending of immigration exclusion and greater access to citizenship. The once-dominant concerns of homeland politics, ethnic community welfare and social programs, struggles against discrimination, and labor organizing gave rise to a broader array of causes and strategies as US-born and new immigrants joined in campaigns to claim greater influence in domestic politics. Asian Americans cultivated ties with mainline political organizations; sought to overcome ethnic differences by developing multiracial coalitions with other Asians as well as black, Latino, and Native American groups; protested war and imperialism abroad particularly on behalf of emerging Third World nations seeking independence; promoted pride in ethnic identity and culture; and advocated for community causes such as educational access, workers' rights, and public health issues. After a century of discrimination and segregation, they demanded greater equality for those whose race, gender, language, immigration status, socioeconomic class, and sexuality had previously limited access to opportunities in America. This broad reform agenda often pitted moderates, radicals, and conservatives in disagreement, even as generational and cultural divides exacerbated internal community conflicts. For all its good intentions and power to inspire and to mobilize, the civil rights movement produced significant gains in the integration of Asians, even as some of its more idealistic agendas remained thwarted by their repositioning as "model minorities."

As early as the New Deal, American-born Chinese and Japanese Americans sought to utilize their citizenship and voting rights to claim attention from Democratic and Republican party organs. The JACL's Mike Masaoka had singular success at the national level in lobbying for Japanese American recuperation with the White House issuing the 1947 Committee on Civil Rights report, *To Secure These Rights*, criticizing the lack of naturalization rights for Japanese Americans among many other serious concerns, the sequence of Congressional legislation granting more equitable citizenship and naturalization rights in the years following, and the mid-1950s systematic abolishing of alien land laws. Political inroads operated at the local level as well. As early as the 1930s, the Chinese American Citizens Alliance recruited voters to support Franklin Delano Roosevelt in San Francisco. Social worker, journalist, and later the first Chinese American postmaster of San Francisco, Lim P. Lee systematically worked within the local Democratic party structure—particularly in aid of the influential Burton family—to wield influence on behalf of Chinese Americans as head of the Cathay Post of the American Legion. Through the 1950s, Lee and other community leaders such as the journalist Dai-ming Lee (no relation) pressed for immigration reform and other measures to normalize the status of Chinese Americans. Lee gained such standing and rapport that in 1966 Phillip Burton, then Representative of California's 5th District, appointed him the first Chinese postmaster of the San Francisco post office. As demonstrated most visibly by Dalip Singh Saund, even without a significant community to serve, Asian Americans operated successfully within party politics to gain government positions.

Perhaps the most sweeping example of Asian political integration was the long-delayed granting of statehood to Hawaii. The territory began applying for statehood in the 1920s, after fulfilling stipulated requirements, but met with opposition in Congress from a staunch core of Southern conservatives who predicted that its majority ethnic-Asian population would surely elect an "Oriental" to serve alongside them in Washington, DC. Cold War politics made such segregationist fears insupportable and Hawaii became the fiftieth state in 1959, after the longest campaign for conversion from territory status. Republican Hiram Fong joined the Senate in 1959, followed by the Democrat Daniel Inouye in 1963. Along with a host of Hawaiian House representatives, they advocated on behalf of Asian American causes, such as redress for incarceration and immigration reform.

Even as new influxes of Asians immigrated under conditions of greater acceptance and opportunities, discriminations from the exclusion era continued to mire many Asian Americans in

8.   In 1964, Chinese American young women campaigned for presidential candidate Lyndon Baines Johnson in San Francisco's Chinatown. They wore LBJ cowboy hats and sashes with "Johnson's Young Miss Team" written in Chinese.

conditions of low pay, long hours, and manual labor, with continued residential segregation characterized by overcrowding, poor sanitation and health measures, urban crime and delinquency, and limited access to education and better employment. Such community problems compelled members of the growing middle class with college educations to challenge the status quo, inspired in part by the black power movement, international and liberationist campaigns abroad, and the antiwar movement at home. Through identity politics, community activism, and cultural transformation, Asian Americans sought to move out of the margins and claim the American mainstream.

Building on the erosion of exclusionary and segregationist laws pursued by moderates working through traditional party politics, the civil rights movement radicalized a vocal minority of both US-born and immigrant Asian Americans who sought to address community needs as framed by both international, local, and multiracial coalitional calls to action, with many inspired by the ideologies and leadership of African American activists. For example, Grace Lee Boggs received a PhD in philosophy in 1940 but faced discrimination in pursuing an academic career. While working in Chicago, Boggs became radicalized and joined the Workers Party. She married the labor activist and auto worker James Boggs, with whom she partnered in organizing and writing about workers and African American rights in Detroit. Yuri Kochiyama experienced incarceration before moving to New York. Living in Harlem, she became politically mobilized upon learning more of black history and culture through the Congress of Racial Equality and got to know Malcolm X, who ideologically linked racism within the US to imperialism in Asia, particularly through the atomic bombing of Japan. Kochiyama was at Malcolm X's side when he was assassinated and remained active as one of the few non-black members in the Republic of New Africa, and the takeover of the Statue of Liberty in 1977 with Puerto Ricans. Other causes included prisoners' rights, nuclear disarmament, and redress for incarceration. Richard Aoki, a Bay Area lecturer in criminal justice, was one of the few Asian American Black Panther Party members to gain a leadership position (although controversially, after his death he was reported to be an FBI informant).

Crucibles of war

In turn, American activists drew inspiration from Asian political and spiritual leaders. The pacifist strategies of Gandhi informed the leadership of Martin Luther King, Jr., while religious leaders such as D. T. Suzuki and Maharishi Mahesh Yogi gained celebrity status and followers such as the Beatles and the actress Mia Farrow. The Black Panthers were influenced by Vietnamese, Algerian, and Palestinian struggles, while Mao Zedong's forceful pronouncements regarding revolution and self-determination, as realized through the then poorly understood mobilization of the Red Guards, voiced the necessity for violent confrontation. Black Panther leaders such as Huey Newton and Bobby Seale distributed Mao's writings as a sourcebook for fomenting revolution through violence and in turn sought to mobilize Chicanos, Puerto Ricans, and Asian Americans in the United States.

A prominent example was the revolutionary, nationwide I Wor Kun (IWK), which emerged from community organizations started by college-educated youth in New York and San Francisco in 1969. Founded under the name LeWays in San Francisco, its members began tutoring programs and afterschool centers to alleviate juvenile delinquency and gang activities. Black Panther leaders contacted LeWays, sharing their readings and discussion groups to encourage formation of the revolutionary Red Guard Party which merged into the IWK in 1971. The IWK published a bilingual newspaper airing Chinatown's social and economic problems, suggested solutions, and offered political analysis, along with meal and health services. Although the CCBA attempted to repress these radical alternatives and challengers for community influence, the IWK persisted and represented leftist perspectives by screening movies and providing information about the PRC in a different perspective from the Nationalist-dominated traditional organizations. The IWK also tackled workers' rights and was active in the anti-Vietnam War movement.

In May 1968, a group of UC Berkeley students formed a coalitional group identified as "Asian American," a concept first named by Yuji Ichioka. The Asian American Political Alliance was founded by Asian members of the Peace and Freedom Party, who sought to emphasize their perspectives in the antiwar and self-determination movements spearheaded by the Black Panthers. Members came from a variety of ethnicities and class backgrounds, including Chinese, Filipinos, and Japanese from all walks of life—working-class, urban, rural, middle-class, immigrant. Some were experienced radicals who had worked with the United Farm Workers or the Student Nonviolent Coordinating Committee. The AAPA evolved into the Asian Community Center (ACC) in 1970, as the college student members enacted their ideals by opening a community center. They circulated leftist information by screening movies and providing literature about the PRC, and opened Everybody's Bookstore in 1970. The ACC distributed free food provided by the Department of Agriculture, published a nutritional newsletter, and provided health screenings, free hearing devices, and glasses. The name changed again to Wei Min She in 1971–1972 (Organization for the People) to evoke commitments to an anti-imperialist, revolutionary stance of a "mass" community-based organization. True to the responsibility they espoused for community affairs, Wei Min She's base was located for a period of time in the International Hotel.

The decade-long struggles to protect the International Hotel brought together a cross section of interest groups by representing several of the most pressing of community issues. Since the 1920s, the so-called I-Hotel had provided low-cost housing and well-frequented communal spaces and services, particularly for cohorts of single men, prevented by exclusionary conditions from marrying or escaping working-class poverty, who had no other home. Many were *manongs*, an affectionate term for older male relatives used for the many Filipino bachelors who were never able to have families of their own. A development company bought the building in 1968, planning to demolish the only home most of its residents could afford in order to install a parking lot serving the nearby Financial District. The confluence of history, working-class rights, housing for the poor, and anti-development concerns motivated a wide coalition of students, community activists, Chinese and Filipinos, and labor organizers to refurbish the building, thereby turning it into an even more central site for community activities, and fight against corporate interests in courts and through demonstrations. Despite these sustained efforts, the San Francisco Sheriff's office enacted a final eviction on August 3, 1977. Two thousand protesters ringed the building outside, linking arms in ranks ten to a dozen deep to forestall the hundreds of riot-equipped police officers charging on horseback who cast aside the demonstrators to reach and remove the remaining tenants. The building was razed but the lot remained unused until construction began on a new low-cost residential project in 2003 with apartments allocated for senior housing, prioritizing the last two surviving *manong* residents of the I-Hotel.

The Katipunan ng mga Demokratikong Pilipino (KDP, Union of Democratic Filipinos) had vigorously defended the I-Hotel as a significant legacy of the history of Filipino Americans. The KDP's agenda extended to the Philippines, where it sought to dismantle the dictatorship of Ferdinand Marcos. International politics engaged many Asian American civil rights activists, with the sovereignty dispute between Japan, the PRC, and Taiwan regarding the Diaoyutai or Senkaku Islands mobilizing many Chinese students and Chinese Americans. The Vietnam War resonated with particular force among Asian Americans, who could see on daily news broadcasts that the hated enemy looked like them. Identification with Third World consciousness and anti-imperialism, which claimed roots in the 1955 Bandung conference, was used to raise awareness of the broader implications of domestic racism and inequalities.

The Third World Liberation Front called upon these principles in bringing together a coalition including the Black Student Union, Latin American Student Organization, Mexican American

Student Confederation, AAPA, Intercollegiate Chinese for Social Action, and Pilipino American Collegiate Endeavor for what remains the longest student strike in US history. Addressing systemic issues of underrepresentation of faculty and students of color across the board, and the paucity of curriculum reflecting their perspectives, the Third World Strike demanded institutional changes that would lead to the founding of ethnic studies as a permanent element of the academy. For five months, from November 1968 through March 1969, protests calling for a broadly based program of ethnic studies and affirmative action immobilized the campus of San Francisco State College. After measures such as calling out the tactical squad of the San Francisco police and arresting students failed to reopen campus, strikers and administrators met to negotiate terms. San Francisco State established the first and only College of Ethnic Studies, whereas other universities such as UC Berkeley, UCLA, and the University of Hawaii began varying configurations of ethnic studies programs or departments, as did many other university and college campuses.

The interdisciplinary field of ethnic studies emerged from the civil rights movement with creative output and scholarly studies acknowledged widely as key components of democratizing American society. Asian American scholars, writers, and artists proactively sought to document and represent the stories and perspectives of their communities with a flourishing of academic and cultural output grounded in anti-imperialist, antiracist ideologies. Arts organizations such as the Kearny Street Workshop, Basement Workshop, Yellow Pearl, *Bridge*, and the *Aiiieeeee* quartet developed performances, music, exhibitions, and publications that explored Asian American identity and cultural claims upon the United States.

Even as Asian American activists sought to make the United States more inclusive of their perspectives, communal experiences, and worldviews, the United States was in the process of remaking

Asian Americans as a model minority group, along a pathway marked by outstanding Asian Americans who attained previously unthinkable accomplishments. The immigrant architect I. M. Pei, for example, received the commission to design the Kennedy Library in Boston in 1964, while American-born Minoru Yamasaki was contracted to design the World Trade Center in 1965. Artists such as Ruth Asawa, Isamu Noguchi, Chang Dai-chien, Shu-chi Chang, and Dong Kingman garnered critical acclaim and lucrative sales. Reforms of immigration law consolidated these gains by encouraging the migration of "brain drain" individuals.

The 1965 Immigration Act rendered permanent the privileging of the kinds of immigrants encouraged by the Cold War. Congress finally dispensed with the Asian-Pacific Triangle and the unequal national origins quotas by imposing uniform twenty-thousand-per-country caps with a seven-category preference system to allocate immigrant visas. Family members received 75 percent, employment immigrants 20 percent, and refugees 5 percent. The emphasis on family reunification was a masked effort to maintain the racial and ethnic composition of the United States, based on the presumption that then dominant populations of European Americans would be the primary beneficiaries. However, the pragmatic realities of economic inequality, political instabilities, and human aspirations have produced migration flows markedly different from that anticipated by Congress. Since 1965, the Asian population has exploded, with those once shut out by race now qualifying through education and employment potential for immigration. Although their numbers far exceed those predicted, the great economic value of the increased Asian immigration—key fodder for the accusation of "brain drain" theft against the United States—has in certain quarters contributed to proclamations of America's successful transformation into a post-racial society.

In 1966, the sociologist William Petersen published the seminal article arguing that quantifiable Asian American attainments demonstrated that racial minorities could gain middle-class prosperity and overcome earlier conditions of exclusion and segregation through hard work, focus on educational and professional milestones, and political conformity, and not through civil rights protests. "Success Story, Japanese-American Style" appeared in the *New York Times Magazine* and identified its title subjects as the ethnic group to have personally experienced the severest racial discrimination, through incarceration. Nonetheless, Japanese Americans had survived and thrived, managing to attain educational and employment levels equal to, and even surpassing, that of native-born whites, according to 1960 census data. Later that year, *US News and World Report* published a parallel article that made similar claims regarding Chinese.

By the 1980s, the preferences enacted with the 1965 Immigration Act had cemented these patterns, importing even more examples of outstanding individually successful Asians and bolstering statistical data that reified Asian Americans as superlative, "model minority" American subjects. Despite their civil rights struggles to remake the terrain of racial and class inequality in the United States, Asian Americans found that through immigration reform and their own aspirations for success, they were playing key roles in new forms of American democracy and multiculturalism, in which they embodied the most effective weapons in the dismantling of the same progressive and affirmative action programs which they had struggled to enact. These ironic contradictions characterize the late twentieth-century integration of Asians into the United States, with the ambivalence of success attained by imprisonment in a gilded cage.

Chapter 5
Imperialism, immigration, and capitalism

Throughout the night of April 29, 1975, tens of thousands of South Vietnamese fled their homes, by air and sea, barely in advance of triumphant communist forces. Most sensationally, the largest helicopter airlift in history evacuated over seven thousand Americans and Vietnamese out of Saigon. Operation Frequent Wind produced wrenching images of America's reluctant final retreat from Vietnamese affairs, conveyed by the heady blend of desperation to escape and the courage and benevolence of Americans in rescuing all too few of their doomed allies. Less visible were the greater numbers of South Vietnamese who had begun self-evacuating days before; those possessing connections and wealth gained seats on planes, but most others launched by boat into the open seas, hoping to be rescued by US ships. In the months following, 138,869 South Vietnamese entered the United States as refugees, a first wave of political immigrants that included many former elites holding the closest ties to the unpopular, US-backed administration of President Ngô Đình Diệm. Between 1975 and 1994, over 1,250,000 Southeast Asians gained admission, mostly as refugees. Sixty-six percent came from Vietnam, 21 percent from Laos, and 16 percent from Cambodia. Joined by later arriving relatives and almost ninety thousand Amerasian offspring of US personnel, Southeast Asian American communities emerged abruptly out of this crisis. Vietnamese Americans eventually became the fourth-largest Asian American group, and one that bore a particularly complicated relationship to belonging in the United States.

More clearly than groups possessing older histories of settlement in the United States, Southeast Asian refugee populations reveal the intersection between US military and imperialist actions overseas with immigration access, and conditions of settlement during the late twentieth century. The United States' quarter-century of both covert and overt interference in Vietnam's fierce struggles for independence from France, and then the civil wars that followed, obligated Americans to help South Vietnamese when the war was lost, including as well the neighboring Laotians, Cambodians, and Hmong whom had been drawn into the conflicts. The United States neglected domestic reform projects in funding its wars in Vietnam, expending billions for weapons, advisors, training, institutional programs, munitions, and troops to combat the popular, but communist, Ho Chi Minh. Through the long, shared struggle against this common enemy, the lives of individual Americans became bound to those of their Southeast Asian allies, whom they had also sought to fortify with American resources, values, and institutions. At its peak in 1968, over a half million American soldiers were stationed in Vietnam, accompanied by extensive support personnel, intelligence operatives, service providers, and administrative staff who required supporting bases and rest and recreation destinations in Hong Kong, Thailand, the Philippines, Taiwan, South Korea, and Japan. As a result of both the Vietnam War and the stationing of US personnel in this belt of military outposts girded to contain the communist threat in Asia, large numbers of Americans lived among Asians, forming friendships, families, and many kinds of working relationships that shaped later migration flows.

The United States' enemy, North Vietnam, became the most fiercely defended place in the world, outspent and out-bombed, and yet nevertheless unrelenting. Its forceful intransigence, along with that of other communist states such as China and North

Korea, contributed to myths of the deviousness and elaborate conspiracies manipulated by totalitarian Asian regimes, anxieties evoked in the 1962 film *The Manchurian Candidate*, which featured the brainwashing of an American, Korean War POW to assassinate the US president so that his stepfather, the vice president, could control the White House.

Despite such paranoid fantasies, and the then-recent history of Japanese American incarceration, political alliances distinguished some Asians as US friends and allies rather than as racially designated enemies. The United States' extended commitment to South Vietnam continued despite widespread public protests and obfuscation by the executive branch of the US government. That such investments of national resources and honor were lost in such a prolonged and dismal defeat left the United States still unable to relinquish its client state, even when it decided finally to officially withdraw in 1973. Two years later, Americans remained a substantial presence through the fall of Saigon. Guilt and disbelief that the United States' show of force had failed to vanquish the communist forces required provision of sanctuary and succor for the hundreds of thousands of South Vietnamese forced to flee their homeland, but also historic amnesia about the the United States' role in intensifying that loss. Unlike its token gestures of relief to the million and a half Chinese refugees in Hong Kong during the 1950s, by 1975 the United States had become too obligated and politically involved with Southeast Asians not to provide significant help. Although a majority of Americans objected to the costs and anticipated disruptions of absorbing so many poor, stateless Asians, President Gerald Ford personally campaigned to promote sympathy and acceptance for this immigrant group.

The high numbers of Southeast Asian refugees admitted, and the urgency of American actions in providing new homes and resources for resettlement, underscored how dramatically the value of Asians to Americans had grown through nearly three decades of the Cold War and its pressures to recruit political allies in Asia and to improve domestic race relations. By 1975, the shared anti-communist cause required support for Asians comparable to that of white refugees, such as the parole of two hundred thousand Cubans in 1960 and 1961. Congress drew upon the legislative template of funding aid for Cuban refugees in enacting the Indochina Migration and Refugee Assistance Act in 1975, which authorized appropriations of $405 million in federal funds to assist in resettling Indochinese refugees by state and local public agencies to meet transportation and refugee expenses, and for employment and training programs.

The second wave of refugees began leaving Southeast Asia in 1978 and were less educated, less likely to be Christian, and were more ethnically diverse, including Chinese, Khmers, lowland Laotians, and Hmong from highland Laos. In flight from communist re-education camps and anti-Chinese campaigns, this wave of immigrants became known as "boat people" for the dangerous and risky means of their escape from Southeast Asia. Many landed in first-asylum countries such as Hong Kong, Malaysia, Thailand, Indonesia, and the Philippines, which quickly became overwhelmed and resorted to expelling refugees, which forced the United Nations High Commissioner for Refugees to enact the Orderly Departure Program (ODP) to manage the outflow and encourage countries such as the United States, France, Canada, and Australia to increase admissions for resettlement. Ethnic Cambodians fled Democratic Kampuchea (DK) as "land people" to refugee camps in Thailand, Vietnam, and Laos to escape Pol Pot's deadly regime and, later, the threat of famine. Ethnic Hmong and other Laotians fled from the Pathet Lao government and sought refuge in camps along the northeastern border of Thailand, where some resided for more than a decade before being resettled or repatriated.

In the United States, the traumas of flight were exacerbated by efforts to distribute Southeast Asian refugees across the fifty states. After initial settlement, however, Southeast Asians relocated in search of more coherent ethnic communities and job opportunities, so that almost 40 percent of Vietnamese Americans now live in California and another 12 percent in Texas. Hmong have congregated in California, Minnesota, and Wisconsin while Cambodians have gathered in Southern California and Lowell, Massachusetts. Some of those from rural backgrounds have sought to return to farming to support themselves. Southeast Asians have also developed new economic niches, such as Cambodian-run doughnut shops or Vietnamese nail salons. Both forms of small business require low initial capitalization, long work hours, and little English while inexpensively providing small-indulgence services. Vietnamese Americans alone make up 37 percent of licensed nail technicians nationwide and dominate 80 percent of the industry in California. Many Vietnamese who remigrated to Texas and Louisiana managed to reclaim former livelihoods fishing along the Gulf Coast, first by working in low-paying jobs on fishing boats and in restaurant kitchens, then by pooling money to buy shrimping boats as independent operators. Their success in these largely family-run enterprises put them into competition with native-born locals, and hostilities ensued through burnings of Vietnamese boats, firebombings, and armed clashes with hooded Klu Klux Klan (KKK) members. In 1981, the Southern Poverty Law Center undertook their case and argued in Houston's US District Court that the KKK was in violation of antitrust protections in seeking to drive Vietnamese from the industry. In winning this case, Vietnamese fishermen gained the protection of the Texas Emergency Reserve as they resumed working.

Despite these inroads into claiming American lives, Southeast Asian Americans have dramatically lower levels of achievement than East and South Asian Americans who immigrate through the selective processes of regular immigration laws, and lower even than national averages. Because they are only 10 percent of the Asian American population, aggregated data masks their lower levels of income, employment, and educational attainment. For example, the poverty rates among the Hmong (37.8 percent), Cambodians (29.3 percent), Laotians (18.5 percent), and Vietnamese (16.6 percent) are much greater than those found among Filipinos (6.3 percent), Japanese (9.7 percent), and Asian Indians (9.8 percent) in 2008. Among Southeast Asians, Vietnamese had the highest median family income at $46,929—an average that was nonetheless 40 percent lower than the per capita national average in 2000.

In comparison, the most highly achieving Asian American group in 2011—Indians—had adult, college-educated rates of just over 60 percent, compared to 55 to 65 percent of Southeast Asian and Pacific Islander adults that had never enrolled in postsecondary education of any kind, and the 40 percent of Southeast Asians that did not complete high school. Unsurprisingly, approximately half of Southeast Asian and Pacific Islander students left college without earning a degree at three to five times the rate of East and South Asians. Given that they are minorities among Asian Americans, these bimodal patterns of attainment and nonattainment are poorly understood much less institutionally addressed, because of pervasive emphasis on the outstanding attainments of Asian Americans as an aggregated group.

Model minorities

A majority of the Asians who have become American did so through less traumatic processes and are widely perceived as "model minorities," whose outstanding educational and economic performance exceed that of even native-born whites. Such levels of attainments stem in large part from the preferences enacted through the 1965 Immigration Act and later legislation, which privilege skilled employees whose qualifications for entry and citizenship rest upon their economic and educational credentials, and employers willing to process applications on their behalf. At the same time, even greater numbers of Asians became able to immigrate through the allocation of more equitable, national caps which now stand at 25,620, including exemptions for immediate relatives of US citizens and certain special immigrants. This annual limit is divided into three main categories at 75 percent for family-sponsored, 20 percent employment-based, 5 percent for refugees, and remaining unused spots for all others, including investors. The overall cap is 675,000, while the employment-based annual minimum limit is set at 140,000, which increases through the addition of unused family-sponsored allocations from the previous fiscal year. Even though this system prioritizes family reunification, because Asian numbers were so low before 1965, a higher percentage of those who have immigrated since 1965 do so through the occupational preferences.

This phenomenon is revealed most strikingly among Asian Indians, who numbered only 12,296 in 1960 but have immigrated at the highest rates since 1965, to more than double their population each succeeding decade to reach 72,500 in 1970, 387,223 in 1980, and 815,447 in 1990. Korean numbers have also increased dramatically, starting from a scant estimated 11,000 in 1960, growing to 69,150 in 1970, 357,393 in 1980, and 798,849 in 1990. Filipino numbers grew from 176,310 in 1960, to reach 343,040 in 1970, and 781,894 in 1980. By 1980, the once second largest population—that is, Chinese—had overtaken Japanese to become the largest ethnic group at 812,178 through immigration, and has remained the most sizable Asian immigrant population.

The influence of employment and investment preferences on once-small populations such as Indians, Koreans, and Filipinos is visible in the early importance of these modes of immigration for these populations: in 1969, 71.8 percent of Indians immigrated through these categories, compared to 34.8 percent of Koreans, and 42.4 of Filipinos. That year, Chinese and Japanese entered through economic preferences at rates of 25.3 and 23.7, respectively. High rates of immigration through employment and investor categories correlates to higher levels of education, and such accumulations of cultural capital tend to carry over through future generations, girding the US-born for higher levels of educational attainment.

Taiwanese immigration illustrates these patterns. Within the ethnic category of Chinese in 1989, Taiwanese immigrated at much higher rates through occupational preferences, at 32.2 percent, compared to those from mainland China at 5.2 percent. According to the 1990 census, Taiwanese Chinese compared favorably to their PRC counterparts in terms of educational attainment, occupation, and income. Sixty-two percent of Taiwanese had completed at least four years of college, as opposed to 31 percent for PRC Chinese and 21 percent for non-Hispanic whites for those aged 25–64. Almost 40 percent of immigrants from China did not have high school diplomas, compared to 8 percent for Taiwan, and 22 percent for Americans overall. The higher socioeconomic profile of Taiwanese Chinese was linked in large part to their immigrant origins. About 70 percent of Chinese across the board were foreign-born but Taiwanese Chinese preponderantly entered under professional or student categories rather than through family reunification categories. For example, 54 percent of China-born immigrants were admitted as immediate relatives of US citizens, whereas only 29 percent of Taiwan-born were immediate relatives of US. citizens. In 1992, the Chinese Student Protection Act permitted an outburst in the numbers of college-educated PRC Chinese by about 54,000, by providing green cards as protection and protest against severe political persecution after the 1989 Tiananmen massacre by the Chinese government.

The ranks of highly educated Asians have grown faster than other groups through the H-1B visa program, which provides additional immigration routes as determined by the needs of US employers. The Immigration Act of 1990 improved access to workers in "specialty occupations," which usually require a bachelor's or higher degree or some other form of certification of work skills, for entry into the United States. H-1B workers include primarily computer professionals, engineers and scientists, financial analysts, management consultants, university professors, researchers, and fashion models of distinguished merit and ability. Initially, H-1B visas were capped at 65,000 plus 20,000 for graduates of US universities, although this number has fluctuated up to 195,000 in some years in response to industry lobbying in Congress. The 2000 American Competitiveness in the 21st Century Act, for example, increased caps while exempting research organizations, institutions of higher education, and other nonprofit entities from the visa cap altogether. To qualify, H-1B workers must have a US company or organization petition the Department of Labor and Homeland Security on their behalf and can be employed for up to three years and opt to extend their stay for another three years. Some H-1B visa holders are eligible to be sponsored or self-sponsored for lawful permanent residence.

In recent years, over 70 percent of H-1B recipients have come from Asia, mostly from India, given that these regions have the higher education infrastructure necessary to train workers, who wield English-language skills that facilitate international business connections in desired fields. Taking these factors into consideration, it is understandable that in 2008 the top four petitioners were Indian outsourcing companies that together received nearly 10 percent of the 109,335 approved visas. In 2009, 48 percent of H-1B recipients were from India, followed by China, Canada, the Philippines, Korea, the United Kingdom, Japan, Mexico, Taiwan, and Pakistan. Together these ten origin countries accounted for more than three-quarters of approved petitions. Nearly 60 percent of H-1B petitions approved were for workers bearing advanced degrees. Although a majority of Asians continue to immigrate through socioeconomically less discriminatory family reunification and refugee categories, the rise in Asian immigration through the H-1B program advanced the overall attainment of Asian Americans into that of super-achievers, even as their ranks expanded in numbers, ethnic and national backgrounds, socioeconomic success, and varieties of immigration experiences. Asian Americans have proliferated in the ranks of the suburban, professional and white-collar middle-class, and many serve in the vanguard of global economic development. Bicultural Asian Americans who hold US educational credentials and networks and experience of US industry are perhaps ideally positioned to advance the globalization of US businesses in partnership with the rapidly developing economies of China, India, South Korea, and Taiwan.

For example, Kanwal Rekhi earned his BS in electrical engineering from the Indian Institute of Technology in Bombay, and then his master's and honorary doctorates in business and engineering from Michigan Technological University. He worked his way through the ranks of various technology firms in Silicon Valley and eventually founded his own firms, most notably in commercialization of the Ethernet, and became the first Indian American to list a venture-backed company on NASDAQ. His interest turned to venture capital and investment in technology start-ups in both the United States and India. Using his wealth, expertise, and networks, Kanwal founded the Kanwal Rekhi Schools of Information Technology at both his alma maters in Bombay and Michigan. He has also, controversially, supported immigration reforms that would reduce family reunification preferences, charging that they allow "low quality" immigration by nonprofessionals such as taxi drivers.

These shifts in overall socioeconomic characteristics had cemented into a widely accepted stereotype by the 1980s. The ascent of Asian immigrants, and particularly Chinese, was signaled by the internationally televised, July 3, 1986 celebration of the centennial of the Statue of Liberty. President Ronald Reagan conferred the one-time honor of Medals of Liberty to a dozen outstanding immigrants. Two and a half of those so celebrated were Chinese: the architect I. M. Pei, the computer scientist and entrepreneur An Wang, and the astronaut Franklin

R. Chang-Díaz, who was also the only Latino through his Costa Rican mother. Six of the remaining honorees were ethnic Jews. By the mid-1980s, Asians were generally seen as overrepresented on the campuses of highly selective universities and colleges—attainments trumpeted in a 1987 *Time* magazine cover story titled "Those Asian-American Whiz Kids" and featuring a cover image of a clean-cut, smiling group of young Asian American students. Jokes circulated that MIT now meant "Made in Taiwan" or that UCLA represented "University of Caucasians Lost among Asians"—jokes which overlooked parallel phenomena that demographically Asians were disproportionately of college age compared to non-Asian groups, and that lower percentages of Asians gained admission to elite institutions seeking to uphold certain conceptions of diversity. High levels of academic attainment also exact costs; Asian American college students experience the lowest levels of happiness and higher than average levels of suicide than their peers.

Residential patterns tend to affirm the image of above-average attainment broadcast by education and employment statistics. Since the 1970s, Asian Americans have been moving into selected suburban areas, not only integrating middle- and upper middle-class neighborhoods but also transforming commercial centers and strip malls through businesses such as supermarkets, restaurants, law firms, dental and medical offices, accounting firms, and insurance agencies. Monterey Park and Daly City in California, and Flushing, Queens are but a few of the most visible Asian American "ethnoburbs," signaling the growing ranks of middle-class Asian Americans. Monterey Park was the first town identified with this kind of new ethnic formation, which generated tensions among older residents who perceived the growing numbers of Asian Americans as a form of takeover, regardless of the affluence and professional standing of their new neighbors. Higher density occupancy, produced by construction of larger houses and townhouses, accompanied by traffic congestion and a proliferation of Asian-language business signs, undermined the

9. The "gates" marking the "Chinatown" shopping district of Austin, Texas, are purely ornamental and not meant to admit pedestrian or vehicular traffic. The structure attracts attention to a large, Chinese Cambodian-owned strip mall featuring businesses run by Vietnamese, Chinese, and Korean Americans such as restaurants, a supermarket, spa services, and candy shops.

benefits of growth accompanying rising real estate values and the reinvigoration of local business districts. During the 1980s, tensions produced backlashes such as proposals for English-only legislation in city councils, even as Asian Americans gained political offices in a city that is now home to a majority of ethnic Asian residents. Judy Chu, for example, has climbed the levels of elected office, moving through positions on the school board and the Monterey Park city council, eventually becoming city mayor, and then the first Chinese American woman elected to Congress, in 2009.

Even as the numbers of suburban Asian Americans have increased, historic urban enclaves have retained their relevance, particularly for Asian immigrants of limited English proficiency who require native-language services, and as tourist districts. New York's Chinatown, in lower Manhattan, has become the largest in the country, providing housing, access to employment networks, and Chinese-language services to immigrants lacking the skills and credentials to enter primary job markets. Some of those most dependent on such ethnic enclaves include the elderly and a significant population of unauthorized, working-age immigrants, who come chiefly from Fujian and Wenzhou and try to make their way in an underground economy of low-paying factory and restaurant work. Ethnic brokers manage these networks to distribute restaurant workers up and down the East Coast, throughout New England, and as far away as Dallas. Immigration businesses and lawyers offer services to help undocumented Chinese try to legalize their status by applying for asylum and other measures. Despite these not always legal dynamics, ethnic enclaves remain vibrant attractions for tourists, alongside other revived historic districts such as San Francisco's Japantown, Los Angeles's Little Tokyo, Seattle's International District, and the Chinatowns of San Francisco, Chicago, Philadelphia, and Boston.

The dichotomies of model-minority success can be seen in the high rates of self-employment among immigrant Asian Americans, particularly among Koreans, at about one-third of that total population. Usually upheld as a staunchly middle-class route to financial independence, displaying attainment of the American dream through hard work, delayed gratification, and perseverance, this form of occupation represents downward employment mobility for college-educated Koreans. Small business owners work take significant risks and work long hours, performing physically demanding labor in businesses such as nail salons, fresh fish stores, take-out restaurants, liquor stores, and green grocers. That so many Koreans undertake this kind of entrepreneurship reflects barriers in the primary job market even for the college-educated. In 1997, 30 percent of Korean Americans aged twenty-five and over had completed four years of college, and many had held white-collar and professional jobs in Korea. They nonetheless came to the United States because the Korean job market for the college-educated is so poor. As immigrants, however, they faced the hurdles of inadequate English-language skills and the inability to transfer their educational credentials and work experiences. Owning a small business represents significant downward mobility for the college-educated, but the best option available under the circumstances. By emphasizing education and attendance at name-brand higher education institutions, Korean second- and third-generations are able to move into the primary labor market of professional and white-collar occupations.

In comparison to other minority groups, Korean Americans have advantages in launching small businesses. They have access to sufficient pools of capital through loans from family and friends, or through rotating credit associations known as *gae*. Some have bought established businesses from relatives, or otherwise draw upon networks for support and advice. They also have access to international import-export chains that allow them to inexpensively import items such as cosmetics and fashion accessories. Many established businesses in poor, ethnic neighborhoods because it was cheaper and they faced less competition from larger, chain corporations, which generally avoided what are considered high-risk, high-crime areas. They provide needed goods and services in underserved neighborhoods, occupying a role labeled by sociologists as "middlemen minorities," in this case sandwiched between whites and blacks.

Through the late 1980s, considerable publicity proclaimed black-Korean tensions, particularly in South Central Los Angeles and New York City, but such accounts oversimplified the complex dynamics. Confounded by how so many Korean Americans acquired businesses in their neighborhoods, some African Americans thought erroneously that Koreans had preferential access to government resources unavailable to them. Koreans were also seen as lacking commitments and meaningful engagements in the neighborhoods where they did business by not living in the same areas, not hiring local residents, and being disrespectful to their customers. Organizations such as the Black-Korean Christian Coalition (1984) in Los Angeles and the umbrella Black-Korean Alliance (1986) did not completely resolve tensions. In 1990, such resentments led to an eighteen-month boycott of a fruit and vegetable market in the Flatbush area of Brooklyn, and a subplot in the Spike Lee movie, *Do the Right Thing* (1989). Tragically, such miscommunications resulted in the March 16, 1991 killing of Latasha Harlins in South Central Los Angeles by Soon Ja Du, for which the latter was acquitted.

Long-standing racial tensions in southern California exploded on April 29, 1992 after the acquittal of four white police officers in the videotaped beating of an African American man Rodney King. Anger about endemic poverty and mistreatment by the Los Angeles police department (LAPD) produced looting and rioting in South Central and Koreatown by local residents, including many Latinos alongside African Americans. Known as *Sa-I-Gu*, Korean for the date, this conflagration of Korean American dreams about prosperity and security in the United States resulted in 16,291 arrests, 2,383 injured, 500 fires, and 52 dead. As the most accessible symbols of longstanding racial hierearchies, Korean merchants suffered almost half of the total property damage—nearly $400 million to 2,300 businesses—even though they also faced limited opportunities and access. Wedged between whites and blacks, their foothold into middle-class, small business success made them the most vulnerable and damaged in ongoing struggles about inequality.

Filipinos, in comparison, lack visibility even though they are the second largest Asian American population. Because they have the longest history of imperial influence from the United States, from the *pensionado* program onward, Filipinos have been oriented toward US institutions and opportunities, made all the more alluring by political instability and economic stagnation in their homeland. English-speaking Filipinos are able to enter the US primary employment market more readily than most other Asians, although they nonetheless suffer downward mobility into service sector jobs. While they are disproportionately college-educated, many work at all levels of the job market, and particularly health provider fields. In residence and employment, Filipinos disappear by absorption into generic areas. Operating fewer ethnic businesses, Filipinos are not associated with historic ethnic districts to the extent of Chinese, Japanese, and now Koreans.

Legacies of exclusion and racialization as foreigners

Greater integration, even as model minorities, has not protected Asian Americans from continued racialization as foreigners, and struggles for greater equality and acceptance thus continued. The legacies of exclusion continued to affect Asian Americans long after legal discriminations had lifted.

In San Francisco's Chinatown during the 1960s and 1970s, concerned parents pursued a decade-long campaign for bilingual education and access. As working-class immigrants living in dense, often unsanitary urban neighborhoods, their children grew up speaking only Chinese. Upon attending public schools, English-only systems thwarted their children's efforts to gain education and socialization because they could not comprehend their teachers or their schoolwork. The San Francisco Unified School District considered integrated classrooms a sufficient measure of equality, regardless of whether Chinese American students were actually learning in those settings. Its prolonged resistance led the community to file discrimination charges in court. This protracted legal process culminated in the Supreme Court's 1974 ruling in the case of *Lau v. Nichols*, citing the 1964 Civil Rights Act, that schools had to provide meaningful services that could be comprehended by all students, requiring bilingual classrooms, textbooks, and teachers. The *Lau v. Nichols* case provides the judicial basis for bilingual access in all areas of government service.

The civil rights movement encouraged Japanese Americans to acknowledge and recover the incarceration era of their history by visiting old camp sites, recording oral histories, and locating and preserving records. At its 1970 annual meeting, the JACL encouraged attendees to press for reparations and in 1980, the National Council for Japanese American Redress filed a class action lawsuit. Under the leadership of legislators such as Senator Danial Inouye and Representatives Sparks Matsunaga and Norman Mineta, Congress opened hearings into incarceration and acknowledged injustice on the part of the US government, and then issued a formal apology and partial restitution through the Civil Liberties Act of 1988.

The civil rights movement's call to celebrate and affirm ethnic cultures flowered during the last decades of the twentieth century. Critical stances, such as that taken by the *Aiiieeeee* team of male authors led by Frank Chin, attempted to identify and celebrate "authentic" Asian American voices as distinct from Asian experiences or those that "pandered" to white audiences. Two of the *Aiiieeeee* group's most criticized authors, Maxine Hong Kingston and David Henry Hwang, have been nonetheless among the most critically acclaimed of Asian American authors through works such as the memoir *The Woman Warrior* and the Broadway play *M. Butterfly*. The success of novelist Amy Tan, whose books are sold through mass market venues such as Costco, opened doors for later generations of Asian American authors like Ha Jin, Jhumpa Lahiri, Susan Choi, Lisa See, and Viet Thanh Nguyen. Asian American characters have featured in perhaps the most mainstream of American entertainments: the primetime, family sitcom, in the form of "All American Girl" (1994) starring Korean American comedian Margaret Cho, and "Fresh Off the Boat" (2015) based on the memoir of Taiwanese American chef-entrepreneur Eddy Huang. Although complaints continue that there are still few roles for Asian American actors, Asian Americans have made inroads in the show business industry as animators, producers, writers, technicians, showrunners, and even directors, including Ang Lee, M. Night Shyamalan, Cary Fukunaga, and Justin Lin, whose commissions now include films featuring non-Asian-specific content, such as Jane Austen's *Sense and Sensibility*, Charlotte Bronte's *Jane Eyre*, and the *Fast and the Furious* series of action films.

Asian Americans seem to have transcended racial categories in other areas of public entertainment. In 1997, the golf phenomenon Tiger Woods claimed his mixed-race, "cablanasian" identity in an interview with Oprah Winfrey, acknowledging his Chinese, Native American, white, and African American father and Chinese Thai mother. Almost all arenas of professional sports now feature Asian American players, including basketball, football, and baseball. The world of high fashion now celebrates Asian designers such as Issey Miyake, Vera Wang, Thakoon Panichgul, and Jason Wu. Integration extends to aesthetics, signaled by Nina Davuluri becoming the first Asian Indian Miss America in 2014.

Globalization produced international superstars such as the martial arts movie star Bruce Lee and the marketing juggernaut "Hello Kitty," as well as creative interplay with the movie worlds of Hong Kong, Japan, Korea, and India. Japanese and Korean pop music infuse American airwaves. Americans also developed tastes for diversifying and increasingly sophisticated versions of Asian food that became available through emerging populations. Established tastes for cheap and convenient Chinese American dishes were supplemented by appreciation for Japanese sushi, Thai pad thai, Vietnamese banh mi, Korean barbeque, and a plethora of regional Chinese cuisines.

Even as objects and persons of Asian origin became mainstream, racialization as foreign and threatening remained uncomfortably and sometimes dangerously ready to surface. In 1982, the brutal death of Vincent Chin brought home the vulnerability of Asian Americans. In Detroit, the auto industry's precipitous decline in the face of stiff Japanese competition set the stage for two white auto workers to engage in a drunken altercation with the Chinese American Chin at a strip club, during which an eyewitness reported hearing one of the white auto workers cry out, "It's because of you motherfuckers we're out of work!" The fight broke up, but Ronald Ebens and Michael Nitz followed Chin after leaving the bar, acquiring along the way a baseball bat that they used to beat him so severely that he died in the hospital a few days later. This shocking act was further compounded when a county judge sentenced Ebens and Nitz to only three years of probation and a fine. The senseless murder and scant consequences mobilized Asian American and civil rights activists, who campaigned for the two men to stand trial for violating Chin's civil rights in committing a racially motivated crime. Although the first federal court convicted Ebens, the next overturned the decision and neither Ebens nor Nitz served any jail time for killing Chin. Chin's mother, Lily, was so devastated by the failure to receive justice for her son that she moved back to China.

Population growth and political participation

Such troubling reminders of ongoing discrimination and limited acceptance stand alongside the growing numbers and visibility of Asian Americans. Of the five main racial groups identified by the Census Bureau, Asian Americans have become the fastest growing, although they are still only 5.6 percent of the US population as of 2010. Between 2000 and 2010, the US Asian population grew 46 percent, compared to Latinos at 43 percent. The 17,320,856 individuals claiming identity as Asian only or in combination with another ethnicity represent tremendous ethnic diversity. The Asian American Pacific Islander (AAPI) racial category consists of forty-eight different ethnic groups located along the full range of the socioeconomic spectrum, from the poor and less educated to the affluent and highly skilled. The five

biggest populations are Chinese (including Taiwanese) at
4,010,114; Filipinos at 3,416,840; Asian Indians at 3,183,063;
Vietnamese at 1,737, 433; and Korean at 1,706,822. The previously
largest Asian group—Japanese—has fallen to sixth largest at
1,304,286. The catch-all category of "Other Asian" includes
Bangladeshis, Bhutanese, Burmese, Cambodians, Taiwanese,
Hmong, Indonesians, Iwo Jimans, Laotians, Malaysians,
Maldivians, Mongolians, Nepalese, Okinawans, Pakistanis,
Singaporeans, Sri Lankans, and Thais, among others, and not
including Pacific Islanders, who are often grouped with Asians.
Three of the five largest groups—Vietnamese, Asian Indians, and
Koreans—had numbered but a few tens of thousands until the
1965 Immigration Act greatly increased the numbers of Asians
who could immigrate, demonstrating the significant impact of
immigration laws upon the size, characteristics, and distribution
of Asian American populations.

Under these new conditions, the Asian American population has
boomed. The end of restrictions on employment and the search
for education have scattered Asians throughout the United States,
as have refugee programs that seek to distribute the impact of
sudden arrivals of poor foreigners. Although historic community
centers in Hawaii, California, Washington, Chicago, and New York
remain the most sizable, new populations such as Vietnamese and
Hmong are now the most numerous in states such as Louisiana,
Alabama, Minnesota, and Wisconsin, brought by government
programs, familiar kinds of economic opportunities in agriculture
and fishing, and the emergence of new community centers. Access
to professional employment in all parts of the country have led
Indians to become the largest ethnic Asian populations in states
such as Texas, Arkansas, Florida, Georgia, North Carolina, South
Carolina, Connecticut, New Jersey, and Michigan. Filipinos are
the most numerous in western states such as Washington,
California, Nevada, Arizona, New Mexico, and Idaho. Chinese are
most numerous only in New York, Massachusetts, Colorado, Utah,
North Dakota, Oregon, and Washington, DC. Of the many who

10. The owners of the Budget Motel, Wichita, Kansas, pose for "The Arch Motel Project" by artist *Pardon My Hindi. According to sociologist Pawan Dhingra, Indian Americans own one of every two motels throughout the United States. A high proportion of these motel owners are Gujaratis surnamed Patel.

are primarily economically motivated immigrants, Asians are dispersed where employment and business opportunities are available—in small-business niches such as motels, gas stations, nail salons, green groceries, liquor stores, doughnut shops, restaurants, and in white-collar fields including medicine, engineering, finance, and the computer industry. Not surprisingly, IT centers such as Silicon Valley, Boston, Seattle, and Austin have comparatively higher levels of middle- and upper-middle class Asian American residents.

Despite the higher than average incomes and levels of educational attainment, the ranks of Asian American voters are disproportionately low. Seventy percent of Asian Americans were born abroad, meaning that nearly two out of every three Asian American citizens gained their eligibility to vote through naturalization. Forty-four percent of Asian American adults have limited English proficiency. As recently as 1996, Asians were only 1.6 percent of votes counted, a proportion that nearly doubled to 2.9 percent in 2012. The Asian American vote has increasingly skewed toward support of Democrats, rising from 31 percent in 1992 and increasing in presidential elections to 43 percent in 1996, 54 percent in 2000, 58 percent in 2004, 62 percent by 2008, and 73 percent for 2012. Nonetheless, Asian Americans are the racial group least likely to identify with a political party.

This lack of definition makes it even more difficult to organize Asian Americans politically. Their relatively low rates of party identification are mirrored by relatively low rates of outreach toward them. In 2012, only 31 percent of Asian American respondents in a survey reported being contacted by a party, campaign, or candidate—far lower than the 58 percent for a nationally representative sample. Asian Americans also upend accepted political wisdom. Asian Indians have the highest median household incomes among Asian Americans and are the most one-sidedly Democratic; Vietnamese Americans, earning one of the lowest median household income levels, support Republicans at some of the highest levels.

Asian Americans Advancing Justice, a civic engagement group, tackles some of the challenges of mobilizing the Asian American vote by conducting outreach, in part by addressing barriers posed by language. In Los Angeles, its local branch partnered with eighteen local organizations to organize the country's largest multilingual phone bank, "Your Vote Matters! 2014," which called voters in seventeen languages—including Arabic, Bangla, Burmese, Cantonese, Mandarin, Khmer, Tagalog, Hindi, Japanese,

Korean, Malay, Urdu, Punjabi, Samoan, Thai, Tongan, and Vietnamese—to encourage voters. As of 2000, 44 percent of foreign-born Vietnamese had become US citizens, the highest naturalization rate of any Asian group, even though Vietnamese had the highest proportion (62 percent) of persons who spoke English less than "very well" at home. Despite their conglomeration into a census category, Asian Americans act very differently at the polling booth, as in so many other arenas of their lives.

Immigrant assets and foreign-born threats

In the aggregate, the employment preferences of the 1965 Immigration Act have closely influenced the characteristics of Asian Americans as a largely immigrant group which is very successful. A 2012 Pew Report found that, "Recent arrivals from Asia are nearly twice as likely as those who came three decades ago to have a college degree, and many go into high-paying fields such as science, engineering, medicine and finance. This evolution has been spurred by changes in U.S. immigration policies and labor markets." Recent Asian immigrants were "about three times as likely as recent immigrants from other parts of the world" to receive their green cards through employer rather than family sponsorship, even though family reunification is still the most commonly used legal status for entry into the United States for Asians. Moreover, those who have chosen to immigrate are grateful for the opportunity to settle amid the greater prosperity and political stability of the United States, so that not only are "Asian Americans... the highest-income, best-educated and fastest-growing racial group in the United States. They are [also] more satisfied than the general public with their lives, finances, and the direction of the country." This celebratory account of Asian American success and integration elides ongoing and pernicious forms of racialization as foreign threats.

In addition to the commonplace microaggressions of being questioned about where one is "really" from, or compliments about

English-speaking abilities, immigrant status or assumptions of being foreign-born or associated with foreign powers present more serious ongoing challenges. Becoming a fully integrated American requires hurdling some stiff barriers, particularly concerning differences of language and recognition of academic and professional credentials. Unlike US degrees, which carry international weight, degrees earned in Asia are often not accepted in the United States so that despite high educational attainments, many immigrants are unable to find commensurate employment through lack of English-language skills or recognized professional credentials.

Asian Americans have been making increasing political inroads, building upon the early successes of Dalip Singh Saund and Mike Matsuoka, although they remain underrepresented in elected political office. San Francisco gained its first elected Chinese American mayor only in 2011, more than 150 years after first settlement. Since 2010, Asian Americans elected to office have included Governors Bobby Jindal and Nikki Haley, Senator Mazie Hirono, Representatives Mike Honda, Doris Matsui, and Tammy Duckworth—the first Thai American and openly lesbian candidate elected to Congress—and Grace Meng, the first Hmong American Congressperson. Both George W. Bush and Barack Obama appointed three Asian Americans to their cabinet: Norman Mineta, Elaine Chao, and Neel Kashkari served under the Republican administration, while Gary Locke, Steven Chu, and Eric Shinseki served in the Democratic one.

Nonetheless, Asian Americans remain readily perceived as suspect foreign agents working on behalf of their ancestral homelands. During the 1980s, anxieties flared as Japanese corporations such as Sony expanded operations and investments in the United States, buying out iconic businesses such as the Rockefeller Center, 7-Eleven, and Columbia Pictures. By the 1990s, the fall of the Soviet Union and China's rise as the United States' chief economic partner and competitor fueled a new wave of "yellow peril" fears.

These spilled over into the political arena in 1996, during the final weeks of the presidential race between Bill Clinton and Bob Dole. The incumbent president was leading heavily when Dole unleashed accusations that communist China had gained undue influence over Clinton's White House through campaign donations made by Asian Americans. The roots of the scandal began with an Indonesian Chinese American staffer in the Democratic National Committee (DNC), John Huang, who had identified Asian Americans as a previously barely tapped source of campaign funds. Through targeted outreach, he brought in over a million dollars in donations, thereby becoming a rising party star. However, before immigrating to the United States through a banking internship in Arkansas where he met the Clintons, the foreign-born Huang had previously worked for the Lippo Group in Indonesia, owned by the ethnically Chinese Riady family, which also had extensive investments in China. When investigations revealed that Huang's donations derived from questionable sources—individuals lacking legal status to donate, or donating above their financial capacities—media reporting magnified the idea that communist China was using this so-called "bamboo network" to exert undue influence over the White House.

The DNC commenced a large-scale investigation of campaign finance practices which investigated only Asian American contributions as potentially suspicious, even though in general campaign donations are rife with influence-buying, with non-Asian foreign interests such as Israel and the French corporation Airbus among the most active of lobbying groups. In this atmosphere of general corruptibility, the problematic donations receiving the most attention were not the largest or the most influential, but those perceived as the most "foreign." The targeting of Asian American donors provided both the DNC, and later the Republican National Committee (RNC), with opportunities to demonstrate their eagerness to crack down on the problem of corrupt fundraising practices, but limited their investigations to this largely insignificant group. Unsurprisingly, campaign fundraising remains an active channel for the buying of outsize and undemocratic influence.

The storms of hysteria regarding the foreign threat posed by immigrant Asians raged again leading into the next presidential election cycle. In late 1999, as Al Gore prepared to run against George W. Bush, the *New York Times* front page trumpeted accusations that the Clinton White House had knowingly allowed a Chinese spy to remain at the top secret Los Alamos research facility, where he had acquired key secrets regarding miniaturized nuclear warheads that had been passed on to communist China.

The accused was Wen Ho Lee, a mild-mannered Taiwanese American mechanical engineer who had arrived for graduate studies in 1965 and had become a US citizen in 1974. Despite the unlikelihood that an ethnic Taiwanese would spy on behalf of China and the deeply flawed evidence and testimony used to argue the case, the subsequent media and political frenzy culminated in Lee's firing from his job and indictment for fifty-nine counts of mishandling restricted information. While awaiting trial, Lee served 278 days in solitary confinement because the FBI persuaded the judge that he had stolen secrets so strategic that the entire nation would be at risk should they fall into Chinese hands.

The espionage case soon fell apart when Lee's lawyer investigated and found that the "top secret" codes Lee was accused of mishandling were outdated and considered merely "confidential," but no longer of significance. The FBI had so exaggerated his guilt and danger that the judge who had ordered his solitary confinement also supervised his release and even apologized for the government's egregious behavior. Despite the improbability and lack of evidence regarding Lee as a master spy serving Chinese interests, in the late twentieth century his racialized foreignness nonetheless played well with the US public and the Clinton administration's goal of demonstrating its stringency against dangers from Asia.

On September 11, 2001, China lost its place as the United States' most likely foreign threat. Simultaneous attacks against the Twin Towers, the Pentagon, and the White House—with the last effort thwarted—left 5,011 dead on American soil through the carefully orchestrated use of commandeered jetliners to bomb these key symbols of US capitalist, military, and political power. The death rate and overall damage far exceeded that of Pearl Harbor, where almost three thousand died and five of eight battleships became inoperable. Shocked and galvanized Americans sought revenge and greater security against these new yet historic enemies, characterized as radical, international, Islamic terrorists, whose clashes against Western Christendom dated back to the Crusades. Al-Qaeda and its leader, Osama Bin Laden, mastermind of the 9/11 attacks, became the focus for national anxieties and aggression, justifying the "War on Terror" which is still being waged, including authorized use of military force (AUMF) in Iraq and Afghanistan, intensified surveillance for terrorist activities, torture and indefinite imprisonment of suspected terrorists, increased deportations, and heightened airport security measures. Islamophobia targets not another nation and its people but a religion attracting a wide range of adherents throughout the world such as Indonesians, Pakistanis, Indians, Chinese Uighur minorities, Filipinos, African Americans, and Arabs from the Middle East, or West Asia. The principle of "military necessity" which sanctioned incarceration of Japanese Americans during World War II is now applied to prisoners of war held at Guantanamo Bay.

Such coercive measures incite ongoing backlash. Even after the death of Bin Laden in 2011 and the withdrawal of US forces from Iraq, a fiercely determined and constantly mutating Islamic resistance continues to combat the War on Terror, now in the form of the Islamic State of Iraq and al-Sham (ISIS), which has issued an international call to jihadists and taken over substantial portions of Iraq, even as fighting continues elsewhere in West Asia and particularly Syria. Like the quagmire of the Vietnam War before it, the United States' protracted war on radical Islam shows no signs of resolving easily, much less providing a conclusive and righteous victory while provoking vast flows of refugees in need of new homes. Meanwhile, the vast majority of Muslims, who are everyday civilians, pursue their lives and livelihoods in constant negotiation against nationalist paranoias that they will be the next undercover agents to bomb the United States. These fears exist alongside the reality of how well many Asian Americans have attained the American dream of immigrant prosperity and stability.

Conclusion

Immigration laws have worked to transform Asian Americans into a laudably high-achieving population. Drawing on census data and a multilingual survey of 3,511 households, the Pew Foundation issued a report in 2012 finding that 74 percent of Asian American adults were foreign-born, with 61 percent of those aged twenty-five to sixty-four having arrived holding at least a BA degree, a level of attainment double that of non-Asian arrivals. In this age range, 49 percent of Asian Americans held university degrees, compared to the national average of 28 percent, earned higher average household incomes of $66,000 compared to $49,800; and 50 percent worked in management, professional and related fields compared to 40 percent in general. The report surmised that almost certainly "recent Asian arrivals [were] the most highly educated cohort of immigrants in U.S. history."

These impressive credentials help to explain why no outcries greeted the news that, in 2009, Asians had become the fastest growing immigrant group in the United States for the first time, overtaking Latinos, who had held the lead since the 1960s. The economic downturn contributed to this shift, which is likely temporary, so that by 2010, 430,000 Asians—or 36 percent of all legal and illegal immigrants—became Americans, compared to 370,000 Latinos at 31 percent. Compared to the 1870s, when a comparative trickle of Asian migration to the West Coast produced the fury of economic competition and racial anxieties that led to Asian exclusion, contemporary acceptance of Asian immigrants reveals how effectively US immigration policies and institutions have developed to fulfill generally held priorities concerning economic competitiveness, national security, and international relations. The threat of Asian immigrants has largely dissipated because immigration laws and bureaucracy now function well enough to maintain their numbers at acceptable levels; and, those who immigrate mostly convey sufficient economic or political advantages for Americans to feel their admission and settlement are justifiable. Even the roughly 10 percent of Asians who have settled without proper authorization do not register as a significant problem in the public consciousness.

The issue of immigration peril has shifted to migrants from across the southern land border, a region that remains impossible for US forces to fully control physically. As the United States' nearest, significantly poorer neighbors, Latino and particularly Mexican migrants are seen as threatening to overwhelm and undermine the United States through sheer numbers and by draining US resources. Resistance to allowing these populations to normalize and gain permanent status remains strong, despite the long history of the shared border, extended periods of gainful employment and tax payments, educational endeavors, mixed-status families, and the many instances in which minor US citizen children are separated from their parents. Unsanctioned entry, employment, and long-term residence now threaten to maintain a permanent group of second-class residents in the United States, even for those arriving as children and thus lacking culpability.

In contrast, Asian Americans, and particularly Chinese and Japanese, were allowed to shed the stigma of illegal status and questioned national loyalties during the 1950s. Present-day immigration controls and remade stereotypes have turned Asian Americans into model minorities whose attainments have been largely attributed to cultural traits which include valuing education, hard work, family solidarity, self-sufficiency, pragmatic economic choices, and political passivity. This image of Asian

American success, attributed to productive cultural values, such as "marriage, parenthood, hard work and career success," has been wielded as a bludgeon against less achieving populations and used to justify the diminishing of social support services and shrinking of public infrastructure for schools. The model minority image seems to verify that the call to "pull oneself up by one's bootstraps" leads to success, if proper discipline and focus are applied, and that failure stems from individual, rather than systemic inequalities. In this narrative of success and failure, the stacking of the deck in favor of Asians selected for demonstrated attainments in education and employability by US immigration laws and practices, disappears. To fully grapple with ongoing conditions of inequality in the United States, intensified by the diminishing of opportunities for upward socioeconomic mobility for the poor and working classes, the agency of government policies and bureaucracies to both restrict but also to selectively promote certain populations must be more fully acknowledged and understood.

References

Chapter 1: Empires and migration

Lafcadio Hearn, "Saint Malo," *Harper's Weekly: Journal of Civilization* (March 31, 1883), http://philipppines.tripod.com/stmalo.htm.

Tatiana Seijas, *Asian Slaves in Colonial Mexico: From Chinos to Indians* (New York: University of Cambridge Press, 2015), 8-25.

Ronald Takaki, *Strangers from a Different Shore* (New York: Little, Brown and Company, 1998), 298.

H. R. Wagner and Pedro de Unamuno, "The Voyage of Pedro de Unamuno to California in 1587," *California Historical Society Quarterly* 2.2 (July 1923): 140-60.

Chapter 2: Race and the American republic

1917 Immigration Act (*An act to regulate the immigration of aliens to, and the residence of aliens in, the United States*), H. R. 10384, 64th Cong. (1917).

Angell Treaty of 1880, November 17, 1880.

In re Ah Yup, 1 Fed. Cas. 223 (D. Cal. Cir. Ct. 1878).

Charles J. McClain, *In Search of Equality: The Chinese Struggle against Discrimination in Nineteenth-Century America* (Berkeley: University of California Press, 1994), 208-210.

Adam McKeown, *Melancholy Order: Asian Migration and the Globalization of Borders* (New York: Columbia University Press, 2008), Chapter 12.

Mae M. Ngai, *Impossible Subjects: Illegal Aliens and the Making of Modern America* (Princeton, NJ: Princeton University Press, 2004), 28-29.

Edward Rhoads, *Stepping Forth into the World: The Chinese Educational Mission to the United States, 1872–81* (Hong Kong: Hong Kong University Press, 2011), 63.

Paul Scharrenberg, "Vital Issues Confronting the California Labor Movement," *Union Gazette* (March 1928).

Herman Scheffauer, "The Tide of Turbans," *Forum* XLIII (June 1910): 616–18.

Aristide Zolberg, *A Nation by Design: Immigration Policy in the Fashioning of America* (Cambridge, MA: Harvard University Press, 2008), 258–267.

Chapter 3: Living in the margins

Vivek Bald, *Bengali Harlem and the Lost Stories of South Asian America* (Cambridge, MA: Harvard University Press, 2013), 6–10.

Carlos Bulosan, *America Is in the Heart* (Seattle: University of Washington Press, 1973), 173.

Linda Espana-Maram, *Creating Masculinity in Los Angeles's Little Manila: Working-Class Filipinos and Popular Culture, 1920s–1950s* (New York: Columbia University Press, 2006), 17.

"Japanese American Creed," *Densho Encyclopedia*, http://encyclopedia.densho.org/Japanese_American_Creed/.

Scott Kurashige, *The Shifting Grounds of Race: Black and Japanese Americans in the Making of Multiethnic Los Angeles* (Princeton, NJ: Princeton University Press, 2010).

Valerie Matsumoto, *Farming the Home Place: A Japanese Community in California, 1919–1982* (Ithaca, NY: Cornell University Press, 1993), 78–84 .

Mae M. Ngai, *The Lucky Ones: One Family and the Extraordinary Invention of Chinese America* (Boston, MA: Houghton Mifflin Harcourt, 2010), Chapters 3 and 5.

Mine Okubo, *Citizen 13660* (Seattle: University of Washington Press, 2014), 54.

Cecilia M. Tsu, *Garden of the World: Asian Immigrants and the Making of Agriculture in California's Santa Clara Valley* (New York: Oxford University Press, 2013), 53, 76, 85, 129, 143–144, 155–156, 175, 206, 207–220.

Chapter 4: Crucibles of war

Eiichiro Azuma, *Between Two Empires: Race, History and Transnationalism in Japanese America* (New York: Oxford University Press, 2005), 119–122.

Charlotte Brooks, *Alien Neighbors, Foreign Friends: Asian Americans, Housing, and the Transformation of Urban California* (Chicago: University of Chicago Press, 2009), 165–166.

Cindy Cheng, *Citizens of Asian America: Democracy and Race during the Cold War* (New York: New York University Press, 2014), 169–170.

Catherine Ceniza Choy, *Empire of Care: Nursing and Migration in Filipino American History* (Berkeley: University of California Press, 2003), 62–67.

Daryl Maeda, *Rethinking the Asian American Movement* (New York: Routledge, 2011), for a succinct overview.

William Petersen, "Success Story, Japanese-American Style," *New York Times Magazine* (January 6, 1966).

Arissa Oh, *To Save the Children of Korea: The Cold War Origins of International Adoption* (Palo Alto, CA: Stanford University Press, 2015), 150.

"Success Story of One Minority in the U.S.," *US News and World Report* (December 26, 1966).

Ellen Wu, *The Color of Success: Asian Americans and the Origins of the Model Minority* (Princeton, NJ: Princeton University Press, 2014), 6.

Chapter 5: Imperialism, immigration, and capitalism

Aseem Chhabra, "Rekhi's Visa Stand Raises a Ruckus," http://www.rediff.com/news/2001/may/10usspec.htm.

Pawan Dhingra, *Life Behind the Lobby: Indian American Motel Owners and the American Dream* (Palo Alto, CA: Stanford University Press, 2012), 1–2.

"Kanwal Rekhi, Managing Director," *Inventus Capital Partners*, http://inventuscap.com/team/kanwal-rekhi/.

Eric Lai and Dennis Arguelles, eds., *The New Face of Asian Pacific America: Numbers, Diversity, and Change in the 21st Century* (San Francisco, CA: AsianWeek, 2003), for statistical summaries.

Wei Li, *Ethnoburb: The New Ethnic Community in Urban America* (Honolulu: University of Hawaii Press, 2008), 101.

Madhavi Mallapragada, *Virtual Homelands: Indian Immigrants and Online Cultures in the United States* (Urbana: University of Illinois Press, 2014), 24.

"NBC News: Asian-American Groups Tackle Language Barriers to Get Out Vote," *Asian Americans Advancing Justice* (November 3, 2014), http://www.advancingjustice-aajc.org/news-media/news/nbc-news-asian-american-groups-tackle-language-barriers-get-out-vote.

Franklin Ng, *The Taiwanese Americans* (Westport, CT: Greenwood Publishing Group, 1998), 44.

"The Rise of Asian Americans," *Pew Research: Social & Demographic Trends*, http://pewsocialtrends.org/2012/06/19/the-rise-of-asian-americans/.

Robert T. Teranishi, "Asian American and Pacific Islander Students and the Institutions That Serve Them," *Change: The Magazine of Higher Learning* 44.2 (2012): 16–22.

"Those Asian-American Whiz Kids," *Time* (August 31, 1987).

US Department of Homeland Security, US Citizenship and Immigration Services. "Characteristics of H-1B Specialty Occupation Workers: Fiscal Year 2011 Annual Report to Congress, October 1, 2010–September 30, 2011." (March 12, 2012): 6–7.

Sam Vong, "Compassion Politics: Indochinese Refugees and the Transnational Politics of Care, 1975–1994." PhD diss. (Yale University, 2013).

Who Killed Vincent Chin? Directed by Christine Choy and Renee Tajima-Pena. Film News Now Productions (1987).

Further reading

Abelmann, Nancy, and John Lie. *Blue Dreams: Korean Americans and the Los Angeles Riots*. Cambridge, MA: Harvard University Press, 1997.

Baldoz, Rick. *The Third Asiatic Invasion: Migration and Empire in Filipino America, 1898–1946*. New York: New York University Press, 2011.

Chan, Sucheng. *Asian Americans: An Interpretive History*. Woodbridge, CT: Twayne Publishing, 1991.

Chan, Sucheng. *This Bittersweet Soil: Chinese in California Agriculture*. Berkeley: University of California Press, 1986.

Chan, Sucheng. *The Vietnamese American 1.5 Generation: Stories of War, Revolution, Flight, and New Beginnings*. Philadelphia: Temple University Press, 2006.

Chang, Gordon H. "China and the Pursuit of America's Destiny: Nineteenth-Century Imagining and Why Immigration Restriction Took So Long." *Journal of Asian American Studies* 15, no. 2 (June 2012): 145–69.

Chang, Gordon H., Mark Johnson, and Paul Karlstrom, eds. *Asian American Art: A History*. Palo Alto, CA: Stanford University Press, 2008.

Daniels, Roger. *Guarding the Golden Door: American Immigration Policy and Immigrants Since 1882*. New York: Hill and Wang, 2005.

Daniels, Roger. *The Politics of Prejudice: The Anti-Japanese Movement in California and the Struggle for Japanese Exclusion*. Berkeley: University of California Press, 1962.

Fadiman, Ann. *The Spirit Catches You and You Fall Down: A Hmong Child, Her American Doctors, and the Collision of Two Cultures*. New York: Farrar, Straus and Giroux, 1997.

Hayashi, Brian Masaru. *Democratizing the Enemy: The Japanese American Internment*. Princeton, NJ: Princeton University Press, 2008.

Hein, Jeremy. *From Vietnam, Cambodia, and Laos: A Refugee Experience in the United States*. Woodbridge, CT: Twayne Publishers, 1995.

Hing, Bill Ong. *Making and Remaking Asian America Through Immigration Policy, 1850–1990*. Palo Alto, CA: Stanford University Press, 1993.

Hsu, Madeline Y. *Dreaming of Gold, Dreaming of Home: Transnationalism and Migration Between the United States and Southern China, 1882–1943*. Palo Alto, CA: Stanford University Press, 2000.

Hsu, Madeline Y. *The Good Immigrants: How the Yellow Peril Became the Model Minority*. Princeton, NJ: Princeton University Press, 2015.

Hune, Shirley, and Gail M. Nomura, eds. *Asian/Pacific Islander American Women: A Historical Anthology*. New York: New York University Press, 2003.

Ichioka, Yuji. *The Issei: The World of the First Generation Japanese Immigrants, 1885–1924*. New York: Free Press, 2006.

Ignacio, Abe, Enrique de la Cruz, Jorge Emmanuel, and Helen Toribio. *The Forbidden Book: The Philippine-American War in Political Cartoons*. San Francisco: T'Boli, 2004.

Jensen, Joan. *Passage from India: Asian Indian Immigrants in North America*. New Haven, CT: Yale University Press, 1988.

Klein, Christina. *Cold War Orientalism: Asia in the Middlebrow Imagination, 1945–1961*. Berkeley: University of California Press, 2003.

Kramer, Paul. *The Blood of Government: Race, Empire, the United States, and the Philippines*. Durham: University of North Carolina Press, 2006.

Lai, Him Mark. *Becoming Chinese American: A History of Communities and Institutions*. Walnut Creek, CA: Alta Mira Press, 2004.

Lee, Erika G. *At America's Gates: Chinese Immigration during the Exclusion Era, 1882–1943*. Chapel Hill: University of North Carolina Press, 2003.

Lee, Erika G. *The Making of Asian America: A History*. New York: Simon and Schuster, 2015.

Lee, Shelley. *A New History of Asian America*. New York: Routledge, 2013.

Lew-Williams, Beth. "Before Restriction Became Exclusion: America's Experiment in Diplomatic Immigration Control." *Pacific Historical Review* 83, no. 1 (February 2014): 24–56.

López, Ian Haney. *White by Law: The Legal Construction of Race.* New York: New York University Press, 1996.

Mabalon, Dawn. *Little Manila Is in the Heart: The Making of the Filipina/o American Community in Stockton, California.* Durham, NC: Duke University Press, 2013.

Miller, Stuart Creighton. *The Unwelcome Immigrant: The American Image of the Chinese, 1785-1882.* Berkeley: University of California Press, 1969.

Okihiro, Gary. *Margins and Mainstreams: Asians in American History and Culture.* Seattle: University of Washington Press, 1994.

Ong, Aihwa. *Buddha Is Hiding: Refugees, Citizenship, the New America.* Berkeley: University of California Press, 2003.

Pascoe, Peggy. *What Comes Naturally: Miscegenation Law and the Making of Race in the United States.* New York: Oxford University Press, 2009.

Patterson, Wayne. *The Ilse: First Generation Korean Immigrants in Hawai'i, 1903-1973.* Honolulu: University of Hawaii Press, 2000.

Prashad, Vijay. *The Karma of Brown Folk.* Minneapolis: University of Minnesota Press, 2000.

Robinson, Greg. *A Tragedy of Democracy: Japanese Confinement in North America.* New York: Columbia University Press, 2010.

Shah, Nayan. *Contagious Divides: Epidemics and Race in San Francisco's Chinatown.* Berkeley: University of California Press, 2001.

Shibusawa, Naoko. *America's Geisha Ally: Reimagining the Japanese Enemy.* Cambridge, MA: Harvard University Press, 2006.

Takaki, Ronald. *Pau Hana: Plantation Life and Labor in Hawaii, 1835-1920.* Honolulu: University of Hawaii Press, 1983.

Tchen, John Kuo Wei. *New York before Chinatown: Orientalism and the Shaping of American Culture, 1776-1882.* Baltimore, MD: Johns Hopkins University Press, 2001.

Vang, Chia Youyee. *Hmong America: Reconstructing Community in Diaspora.* Urbana, IL: University of Illinois Press, 2010.

Yoo, David, ed. *New Spiritual Homes: Religion and Asian Americans.* Honolulu: University of Hawaii Press, 1999.

Further reading

Index

9/11, 141–42
Thirteenth Amendment
  see constitution, US
Fourteenth Amendment
  see constitution, US
442nd Regimental Combat Team,
  84–85, 88, 100

A

Abiko Kyutaro, 21, 43–44, 63, 72–73
acculturation, 3–5, 43–45, 57–59,
  61, 68–69, 76–78
activism, civil rights, xviii, 38, 44,
  61, 66–67, 88, 106–107, 110–13
  see also civil rights movement;
  court, activism; workers,
  organized
adoption, international, 102–103
African Americans, xviii, 4–5, 27,
  28, 30–32, 36, 46, 56, 62, 68,
  101, 105, 106, 109, 110, 112,
  129–30, 133, 142
agriculture, 8, 11–12, 14, 16, 19,
  21–22, 25, 43–44, 50–53,
  60–66, 78, 80, 87–88, 90, 120,
  135 *see also* plantations
Aiiieeeee, 113, 132
alien land laws, 43–46, 52–53, 78,
  91, 106

Angel Island, 36–37, 48
Angell Treaty (1880), 34–35
  see also treaties, unequal
Aoki, Richard, 109
Asawa, Ruth, 114
Asian American Pacific Islander
  (AAPI) category, 134
  see also identity, Asian
  American
Asian American Political Alliance
  (AAPA), 111, 113
Asian Americans Advancing
  Justice, 137–38
Asian-Pacific Triangle, 91, 99, 114
assimilation/nonassimilation, xviii,
  23–26, 29, 45, 47–48, 54, 83–86,
  88, 90–91, 94–96, 100–103,
  107–109, 126 *see also* citizenship

B

Back to Bataan, 100
Bandung Conference, 112
Bangladesh/Bangladeshis, 4,
  96, 135
Bengalis, 22–23, 26, 61–62
Bhutanese, 135
Bigler, John, 30
Black Americans *see* African
  Americans

Black-Korean Alliance *see Sa-I-Gu*
Black-Korean Christian Coalition
    see Sa-I-Gu
Black Panthers, 109–11
black power movement *see* civil
    rights movement; coalitions,
    interethnic
Boggs, Grace Lee, 109
"Bonanza", 65
brain drain, 99, 105, 114 *see also* H-1B
    visa program; immigration,
    selection; workers, skilled
Brando, Marlon, 101
Brintnall, Caleb, 6–7, 15
brokers, 2, 12–13, 20–22, 39, 57–58,
    64, 66–67, 76
brotherhoods *see* organizations,
    fraternal
Buck, Pearl, *The Good Earth*, 47,
    63, 69, 102
Buddhism *see* organizations,
    religious
Bulosan, Carlos, 64–65
Bunker, Chang and Eng
    see Siamese Twins
Burke, Thomas, 67
Burlingame Treaty (1868), 27, 34
Burma/Burmese, 11, 12, 89, 96,
    135, 137
Bush, George W., 139
businesses, small, 19, 20, 21–22, 39,
    64, 65, 68, 69–70, 88, 104,
    120, 126, 128–29, 136

C

Caballeros de Dimas-Alang, 66, 73
Cable Act *see* laws, immigration
California, 1, 7, 9, 10–11, 18–22,
    26–27, 30–33, 36–37, 39,
    41–47, 50, 52, 56–57, 63–66,
    68–74, 76–81, 107–108,
    110–12, 120, 126, 128, 130–31,
    135, 139
Cambodia, 12, 89, 96

Cambodians, 116, 117, 119, 120–21,
    127, 135, 139
Campaign Finance Scandal,
    140–41
Canada, 11, 16, 25, 74, 119, 124
capitalism, xvii, 2, 5–6, 8, 11–14, 16,
    19, 22, 98, 111–12, 114, 116,
    123–25, 136, 139, 144
Caribbean, 6, 8, 11, 23, 61
Castillo, Toribio, 80–81
Chan, Charlie, 63
Chang, Dai-chien, 114
Chang-Diaz, Franklin, 126
Chang, Shu-chi, 114
Chao, Buwei Yang, *How to Cook
    and Eat in Chinese*, 100
Chao, Elaine, 139
Chavez, Cesar, 76
Chen Yixi (Chin Gee Hee),
    66–67
Chiang Kai-shek, 94
Chiang Kai-Shek, Madame,
    89–90
China, xix, 6–7, 9, 11–14, 17–18, 20,
    29, 32, 34, 36, 38, 59, 67, 75,
    88–89, 91–92, 94–95, 102, 112,
    117–18, 123, 125, 139–41
China Daily News, 76
China Lobby, 94
China trade, 1, 6–7, 9, 11–12, 15, 20,
    34, 67–68, 139
Chinatowns, 22, 57–58, 67–69, 71,
    108, 110, 127–28, 131
Chinese, 5, 7, 9, 11–14, 16, 18–23,
    25–29, 30–41, 53–60, 62–73,
    75–81, 89–98, 100, 104,
    106–108, 110–13, 115,
    118–19, 122–28, 131–35,
    139–42, 144
Chinese American Citizens Alliance
    (CACA), 59, 77, 107 *see also*
    organizations, US-born
Chinese Consolidated Benevolent
    Association (CCBA), 36,
    67–68, 110

Chinese Educational Mission, 19–20
    see also Yung Wing
Chinese exclusion laws, 34–37, 40
    see also laws, immigration,
    1882 Chinese Restriction Act
Chinese Students Monthly, 73
Chin, Frank *see Aiiieeeee*
Chin, Vincent, 133–34
Cho, Margaret, "All American
    Girl", 132
Choi, Susan, 132
Christianity, 4–8, 17, 21, 30, 32, 89
Chu, Judy, 127
Chu, Stephen, 139
Chung Sai Yat Po (Zhongxi
    ribao), 72
citizenship, xviii, 18, 23, 27–30,
    32–33, 37–38, 40, 45–47, 51,
    69, 76–78, 81–85, 89–91,
    105–106, 136–38, 141, 144
Civil Liberties Act 1988, 132
civil rights movement, xviii,
    106–13, 115, 131–34
Clinton, Bill, 140–41
clipper trade, 2, 6
coalitions, interethnic, 18, 19, 56,
    63–64, 66–70, 76, 80, 89,
    105–106, 109–12, 130
Cold War, xviii, 83, 88–104, 107,
    114, 116–19
Coloma, Frank, 42–43
communism, hostility to, 94–95,
    97–99, 110, 116–19,
    140–41
compatriotism *see* organizations,
    native-place
competition, economic, 5, 27, 32,
    60, 76, 78, 120, 129
Confession Program, 95
conflict, interethnic, 14, 60, 75–76,
    80–81, 129–30
constitution, US, 30, 32, 37
Cook, James, 6
coolies *see* workers, coerced and
    contract

court activism, 134
    challenges regarding citizenship,
        33, 37–38, 45–46,
    challenges to immigration
        enforcement, 36–37
    challenges to incarceration, 79,
        85–86
    challenges to segregation, 41–42,
        58, 131–32
    Ho Ah Kow v. Nunan, 32
Cruz, Philip Vera, 76 *see also*
    agriculture; workers, organized
Cuba/Cubans, 8, 13, 17, 25, 99, 119

D

da Unamuno, Pedro, 1–2
Daly City, 126
Davuluri, Nina, 133
Dayal, Har, 74–75
de Gama, Vasco, 11
Dhingra, Pawan, 136
Diaoyutai movement, 112
diaspora, 8–13, 16–17, 60, 74
Dillingham Commission, 47
    see also race/racism
discrimination, employment, 30,
    31, 42–45, 61, 64, 78–79,
    87–88, 106–108
Dole, Robert, 140
Dong Kingman, 96, 114
Do The Right Thing, 130
Du, Soon Ja, 129
Duckworth, Tammy, 139

E

Ebens, Ronald, 134
education, xix, 5, 7–8, 18, 20–21,
    26, 41, 45–46, 49–50, 59–60,
    65, 72, 78, 81–82, 84, 87,
    96–98, 103–106, 108–109,
    114–15, 121, 125, 129, 131–32,
    135, 137, 139, 144–45
    see also exchange programs

Eisenhower, Dwight D., 97, 99
empire, xvii, 6–7, 12–14, 106
    British, 5–6, 12, 22, 74–75, 96
    French, 5, 12, 95, 117
    Japanese, 14, 16–17, 29, 39, 46,
        60, 74, 81, 95
    Portuguese, 3–5
    Spanish, 1–5, 16–17, 19
    US, 12, 16–17, 40, 49–51, 95–97,
        100, 102, 109, 117–18, 130, 142
Endo Mitsuye, 79, 86 see also court,
    activism
"enemy aliens", 53, 55, 78, 81, 88, 91
Espana-Maram, Linda, 70
ethnic studies, 113
ethnoburbs see Chinatowns
Ex parte Mitsuye Endo see court
    activism
exchange programs, 91, 95–98
Exchange Visitor Program
    (EVP), 98
exclusion, Asian, xviii, 26, 29–42,
    46–51, 89, 93, 105, 107–109,
    111, 131
exempt classes see immigration,
    enforcement; laws,
    immigration
explorers, xvii, 1–2
eugenics see race, racism

F

families, xviii, xix, 5, 9, 14, 25, 39,
    41–46, 52–59, 62–65, 72–73,
    78–79, 87–91, 95, 99–101, 105,
    109, 111, 114–17, 120–22, 129,
    144–45
Federal Bureau of Investigation
    (FBI), 95, 109, 141
Filipino Federation of America, 74
Filipinos, 1–2, 5, 16–18, 20, 22–23,
    41–42, 49–51, 54–57, 63–66,
    70–74, 76, 80–81, 90, 93, 98,
    100–101, 104–105, 111–13,
    121–22, 124, 130–31, 135, 142

Fishel, Wesley, 97
fishing and shrimping, 2, 5, 8, 10,
    16, 19–22, 25, 50, 63–64,
    120, 135
Flower Drum Song, 100
Flushing, Queens, 126
Fong, Hiram, 107
Fong Yueting v. US see court
    activism
Ford, Gerald, 119
Fu Manchu, 63
Fukunaga, Cary, Jane Eyre, 133
Fulbright Act see exchange
    programs
Furuya Masajiro, 67, 70

G

Gadar Party, 74–75
Galleon trade, 1–4, 15
Gandhi, 110
Gentlemen's Agreement (1907),
    39–40
Ging Hawk Club competition,
    59–60
Go for Broke!, 85, 100
Golden Hills News (1853), 72
Gold Rush, 1, 18–20
Gong Lum v. US see court activism
Good Earth, 63
Grant, Ulysses S., 33
Guantanamo Bay, 142

H

H-1B visa program, 123–25
Ha Jin, 132
Haley, Nikki, 139
Hannah, John, 97
Harlins, Latasha, 130
Hawaii, 6–9, 11–18, 21–22, 40–49,
    60, 62, 64, 81, 84, 107, 135
Hawaiian Sugar Planters
    Association (HSPA), 9, 13,
    16–17

Hawaiians, 6–7, 9, 13–14, 107
Hayes, Rutherford B., 34
Hearn, Lafcadio, 5
Heart Mountain, 79
Hello Kitty, 133
Hill, James J., 67, 70
Hirabayashi, Gordon, 79, 86
Hirabayashi v. US see court
    activism
Hironata, Katie, 86–87
Hirono, Mazie, 139
Hitler, Adolf, 90
Hmong, 117, 119–21, 135, 139
    see also Cambodians
Ho Chi Minh, 117
Hollywood, 63, 69, 86, 89–90,
    100–101, 110–11, 118, 130,
    132–33
Honda, Mike, 139
Hong Kong, 10, 11, 15, 18, 20, 22,
    67, 98, 101, 117–19, 133
Hooper, William, 9, 12
Hopu, Thomas, 7–8, 15
Huang, Eddy, "Fresh Off the
    Boat", 132
Huang, John, 140
Hwang, David Henry, *M. Butterfly*,
    132

I

I Wor Kun (IWK), 110
Ichioka, Yuji, 111
identity, Asian American, xvii, xix,
    54–55, 110–11, 113, 126,
    132–38
immigrants, unauthorized, xviii,
    35–36, 38, 49, 58, 67–69, 95,
    128, 143–44
immigration
    enforcement of, 35–41, 48–49,
    57–58, 82, 93–95, 98, 124,
    143–44 *see also* Angel Island
    European, 8, 23–24, 26, 30,
    47–48, 71, 92

family reunification and, 41, 43,
    55–56, 91, 95, 101–105, 114,
    116, 122, 125, 138
restriction, xviii, 27, 29–42,
    46–51, 53, 90–91, 125
selection in, xix, 29, 41, 47, 88,
    91–95, 98–99, 103–105, 114–15,
    121–25, 135, 138, 143–44
    see also H-1B visa program
imperialism *see* empire
incarceration, 55, 78–84, 86–88,
    94, 104, 109, 115, 118,
    132, 142
independence movements, 17,
    73–74, 89, 95–96, 106, 109,
    110, 116 *see also* nationalism
India, xix, 3–4, 10–12, 15, 29, 42,
    89, 124, 133
Indian Institute of Technology, 125
Indians, 11, 22–23, 38, 41, 46, 61,
    63, 74, 90, 93, 97–98, 121–22,
    124, 133, 135–37, 143
Indonesia, 4, 12, 41–42, 89, 96,
    119, 140
Indonesians, 135, 140, 142
Ing Hay, 20–21, 55
Inouye, Daniel, 107, 132
Ishikawa, Suetsugu, 52–53
Itliong, Larry, 76

J

Japan, xix, 4–5, 14–17, 21, 29,
    39–40, 43, 47–48, 60, 62, 66,
    78, 81, 84, 88–89, 94, 96,
    101–102, 109, 112, 117, 133
Japanese, 14–16, 18, 20, 23, 26,
    38–40, 43–46, 52–57, 59–60,
    62–67, 69–70, 72–73, 75–89,
    91, 93–95, 97, 101–102,
    105–106, 111, 115, 121–22, 124,
    131–33, 135, 142, 144
Japanese American Citizens League
    (JACL), 77, 82, 84–86, 91,
    106, 132

Japanese Association of America (JAA), 43, 66, 75, 77
Japantowns/Nihonmachi/Little Tokyo, 69–70, 128, 131
Jindal, Bobby, 139
Johnson, Lyndon B., 108
journeys, xvii, 1, 2, 6, 9–10, 27, 29, 62
Judd, Walter, 90

K

Kamehameha, 7
Kanemoto, Hatsu, 52–53, 59, 79, 87
Kang Youwei, 75
Kashkari, Neel, 139
Katipunan ng mga Demokratikong Pilipino (KDP, Union of Democratic Filipinos), 112–13
Kawahara, Katsusaburo, 62, 69, 80
Kearny Street Workshop, 113
Kennedy, John F., 99, 114
Khmers, 119 *see also* Cambodians
kibei, 60, 84
King, Martin Luther, 110
King, Rodney, 130
King and I, The 100
Kingston, Maxine Hong, *The Woman Warrior*, 132
Kochiyama, Yuri, 109
Korea, xix, 16–17, 29, 88–89, 94, 96, 117–18, 125, 133
Korean National Association (KNA), 74
Korean War, 88, 94, 102, 118
Koreans, 16–17, 20, 22–23, 34, 55, 63, 74–75, 77, 93, 95–98, 101, 103–104, 122, 124, 127–32, 135
Korematsu, Fred, 79, 86
K-pop, 133
Ku Klux Klan, 120
kulis see workers, coerced and contract
Kwan, Nancy, 100–101

L

labor *see* workers
labor unions *see* workers, organized
Lahiri, Jhumpa, 132
languages, varieties, xix, 18, 61, 72–73, 84, 120, 124, 127–31, 137–39
Laos, 12, 96, 116, 119
Laotian, 117, 119, 121, 135
Lau v. Nichols see court activism
laundries, 19, 21, 56, 65, 75 *see also* businesses, small
laws, immigration and citizenship
    1790 Nationality Act, 26, 30, 32, 44
    1862 "An act to prohibit the 'coolie trade' by American citizens in American vessels,", 27
    1875 Page Act, 33–34
    1882 Chinese Restriction Act "An Act to execute certain treaty stipulations relating to Chinese", 34–35
    1917 Barred Zone Act, 40–42
    1921 Emergency Quota Act, 47
    1924 Johnson-Reed Immigration Act, 18, 46–48
    1934 Tydings-McDuffie Act, 50–51
    1946 Luce-Celler Act, 90
    1948 Displaced Persons Act, 92 *see* refugees
    1952 McCarran-Walter Immigration Act, 26, 53, 91, 94, 98, 105
    1953 Refugee Relief Act, 92, 99, 103 *see also* refugees
    1962 Public Law, 87–88, 99 *see also* immigration, selection
    1965 Hart-Celler Immigration Act, 48, 99, 103–105, 114–15, 121–22, 135–36, 138

1975 Indochina Migration and Refugee Assistance Act, 119 *see* refugees

1992 Chinese Student Protection Act, 123 *see* refugees

Lee, Ang, *Sense and Sensibility*, 133

Lee, Bruce, 133

Lee, C. Y., 100 *see also Flower Drum Song*

Lee, Dai-ming, 107

Lee, Lim P., 107

Lee, Rose Hum, 59

Lee, Sammy, 96

Lee, T. D., 92

Lee, Wen Ho, 141

Lin, Justin, *Fast and the Furious*, 133

Little Manilas, 70–71

Locke, Gary, 139

Loomis, A. W., 57

Loyalty Registration (1943), 83, 87, 95

lumber, 2, 10, 20–22, 38, 63, 67

Lung On, 20–21, 55

Luzon Indians *see* Filipinos

M

MacArthur, General Douglas, 88

McCarthy, Joseph, 94

McWilliams, Carey, 81

Mahareshi Mahesh Yogi, 110

"Malay", 42

Malaysia/Malaysians, 4, 11, 12, 25, 89, 96, 119, 135

Malcolm, X, 109

Manchurian Candidate, 118

Manila Men, 5

Manzanar, 79

Mao Zedong, 94, 110

Marcos, Ferdinand, 112

Masaoka, Mike, 82–83, 85, 88, 106

Matsui, Doris, 139

Matsunaga, Sparks, 132

Meng, Grace, 139

merchants, xvii, 2, 8, 11–13, 18, 20, 34, 38–39, 41, 49, 57, 67–69, 75, 130

Mexicans, 30, 48, 56, 59, 76, 79, 81, 93, 144

Mexico, 3–5, 9, 11, 15, 17, 30, 40, 56, 124

Michener, James, 100–101

Michigan State University Vietnam Advisory Group program (MSUVAG), 97–98

"middlemen minorities", 129–30

"military necessity", 78, 82–84, 86–87, 142

military service, 2, 11, 46, 51, 64, 75, 77, 81–82, 85–86, 88, 90–91, 94–95, 96, 101–102, 104–105, 117, 141–42

Mineta, Norman, 132, 139

mining/miners, 2, 18–19, 20

miscegenation, 5, 25, 30, 41–42, 50–51, 56, 62, 100–102, 105, 109, 116–17, 153

missionaries, xvii, 2, 5, 7–8, 17–18, 29, 34, 41, 57, 90, 94, 102

mixed race *see* miscegenation

Miyake, Issey, 133

"model minority", xix, 89, 99, 105–106, 114–15, 121–26, 128, 138–39, 142–45

"Mongolian", 31, 33, 42, 56, 58

Mongolians, 135

Monterey Park, 126–27

Mori Arinori, 21, 26

Muslims, 142–43

N

Nast, Thomas, 28

National Japanese American Student Relocation Council, 87

nationalism, xvii, 14, 17, 25, 49, 60, 72–75, 84–85, 89, 95–96, 105–106, 143

Nationalist Party (China, Taiwan), 72, 75, 91, 94, 110

National Japanese American Student Relocation Council, 87

Native Americans, xviii, 1, 7

nativity, US, 37–39, 44, 52–54, 56, 58–60, 77–79, 83–86, 100–101, 104, 109, 115, 121, 129 *see also kibei*; *Nisei*; *Sansei*

Nepalese, 135

New York, 6–7, 10, 15, 22–23, 56, 59, 61, 68, 83, 109–10, 128, 135

newspapers, ethnic, 21, 61, 66, 72–73, 77, 84, 110

Newton, Huey, 110

New York, 6–7, 10, 15, 22–23, 56, 59, 61, 68, 83, 109–10, 128, 135

Ng Poon Chew, 72

Ngô Đình Diệm, 97, 116

Nguyen, Viet Thanh, 132

Nichibei Shimbun, 21, 72–73 *see also* newspapers, ethnic

Nitz, Michael, 134

Noguchi, Isamu, 114

"no-no boys", 83, 85

O

Obama, Barack, 139

Okubo, Mine, *Citizen 13660*, 78–80, 83–85

opium, 12, 13, 20, 32, 43, 68

'Opukaha'ia, 6–7, 15

organizations,
    fraternal, 57, 66, 72–75, 77
    native-place, 54–56, 70–72, 128
    religious, xix, 17, 29, 45, 73, 77, 87, 110, 142
    US-born, 76–77, 109–11

Ozawa v. US see court activism

P

"pachuke", 85

Page Act *see* laws, immigration

Pakistan/Pakistanis, 96, 124–25, 142

paper sons *see* immigrants, unauthorized

Park Yong-man, 75

Pearl Harbor, 47, 79, 142

Pei, I. M., 92, 114, 126

pensionadoes, 49–50, 64, 96, 130 *see also* students; education

People's Republic of China (PRC) *see* China

Petersen, William, 114–15

Pew Report (2012), 138, 143

Philippines, 1–4, 11–12, 15, 17, 29, 40, 42–43, 49–50, 64, 66, 73, 96, 102, 112, 117, 119

Philippines Review, 72

picture brides, 39, 43, 54, 55, 73, 78 *see also* families

Pilipino American Collegiate Endeavor, 113

plantations, 2, 5, 8–10, 12–14, 16–18

politics, electoral, 33, 77, 90, 106–108, 127, 137, 139–41

Pol Pot, 119

Poston, 79

prostitution, 33–34, 41, 43, 101–102

Protect the Emperor Society, 75

Punjabis/Sikhs *see* Indians

Q

Qing dynasty, 13, 75

R

race/racism, xviii, 6–7, 24–26, 28–30, 33, 40, 45–47, 50, 64–65

Rafu Shimpo, 72, 77

railroads, 2, 19, 22, 27, 29, 35, 57, 63, 66–67, 69–70

Reagan, Ronald, 125–26

Reciprocity Treaty, 9 *see also* treaties, unequal

Red guards *see* Mao Zedong

redress, 107, 132

refugees, 91–92, 97–100, 102–103,
    114, 116–20, 122, 124, 135, 142
Rekhi, Kanwal, 125
Repeal, Chinese exclusion, 38
representations, movie, *see* Hollywood
restaurants, ethnic, 19–20, 21, 23,
    63, 65, 69, 70, 104, 120,
    126–28, 133, 136
    see also businesses, small
Rhee Syngman, 74–75, 96
Rivera, Diego, 79
Rizal, José, 73
Rock Springs massacre, 35
Rodgers and Hammerstein, 100–101
Roldan, Salvador, 41–42
Roosevelt, Franklin D., 79, 107
Roosevelt, Theodore, 38–39
Royal Hawaiian Agricultural
    Society (RHAS) *see* Hawaiian
    Sugar Planters Association

S

Sa-I-Gu, 129–30
sailors, xvii, 1–2, 5, 12, 23
Sakauye, Eiichi, 53, 87–88
San Francisco State College, 113
San Juan, Catarina de, 3–5, 15
Sansei, 88, 105
Saund, Dalip Singh, 90, 96, 107, 139
Sayonara, 101
Seale, Bobby, 110
secret societies *see* organizations,
    fraternal
See, Lisa, 132
segregation, xviii, 24, 31–39, 41–42,
    53, 56, 58–59, 88, 89, 107–108
servants/domestic service, 4, 19,
    21–23, 43, 65
Shima, George, 22, 43–44, 63, 66
Shinseki, Eric, 139
Shyamalan, M. Night, 133
Siam *see* Thailand
Siamese Twins (Chang and Eng
    Bunker), 25–26, 32, 51

Singapore, 4, 11–12, 74, 135
slavery, 3–5, 23
    chinos/Asian slaves, 34–35
Smith-Mundt Act *see* exchange
    programs
Sone, Monica, *Nisei Daughter*, 100
Soong, Meiling *see* Chiang
    Kai-shek, Madame
Southern Poverty Law Center, 120
South Pacific, 100
Sputnik, 99
Statue of Liberty, 125–26
"stranded students", 91–93, 100
    see also immigration,
    selection; refugees; students;
    workers, skilled
students, 2, 7, 18–22, 26, 34, 37–39,
    41, 45–46, 63–65, 73, 78, 80,
    87, 90, 93, 96–97, 103–104,
    123, 126, 141
Sun Yat-sen, 72, 75
Suzuki, D. T., 110

T

Taft, William Howard, 49
Tagore, Rabindranath, 41
Taiwan, 14, 16, 89, 97–98, 102, 112,
    117, 125
Taiwanese, 123–26, 132, 135, 141
Takahashi, Charles Tetsuo, 67
Tan, Amy, 132
Tape family, 57–59, 61
Tape v. Hurley *see* court activism
Teahouse of the August Moon, 100
Thailand, 12, 25, 42, 101–102,
    117, 119
Thais, 25–51, 133, 135
Thakoon Panichgul, 133
Thind v. US *see* court activism
Third World Liberation Front,
    112–13
Tiananmen Massacre, 123
tongs *see* organizations, fraternal
Topaz, 79–80

To Secure These Rights, 106
tourism, 23, 61, 68–71, 101, 128
trade, xvii, 1–3, 6, 12, 18–20, 23, 25, 51, 61–62, 67–70, 129
Transcontinental Railroad, *see* railroads
transnationalism, 13–14, 16, 18–19, 46, 55–56, 60–62, 66–67, 70, 72–75, 112, 134, 139–41
treaties, unequal, 9, 12, 14, 34–36
Treaty of Guadalupe Hidalgo (1848), 9, 30 *see also* treaties, unequal
Treaty of Nanjing, 12 *see also* treaties, unequal
Treaty of Kanghwa, 16–17 *see also* treaties, unequal
Truman, Harry, 91, 99
Tule Lake, 79, 83

U

UC Berkeley, 21, 45, 79–80, 110, 113
UCLA, 113, 126
Umeki, Miyoshi, 100–101
United Nations (UN), 94, 96, 119

V

vice and Asian Americans, 32, 43, 50, 57, 68
Vietnam, 12, 89, 96–97, 101–102, 116–19
Vietnam War, 97, 102, 110, 112, 116–19, 142
Vietnamese, 97, 101–102, 110, 116–21, 127, 135, 137–38
violence, anti-Asian, 31, 33, 35, 38, 50, 67, 81, 112, 120, 130, 133–34

W

Walter, Francis, 92
Wang, An, 92–93, 104, 125
Wang, Vera, 133

war brides, 88, 101, 103, 105
War on Terror, 142
War Relocation Authority (WRA), 79, 86–87
Wei Min She, 111
Winfrey, Oprah, 133
Wong Chin Foo, 72
Wong, Jade Snow, *Fifth Chinese Daughter*, 96, 100
Wong Kim Ark v. US see court activism
Woods, Tiger "Cablanasian", 133
workers, 8–14, 16–24, 27, 34, 44, 50, 60, 62, 64, 76, 79, 81, 87, 128
    coerced, xvii, 1–2, 3–5, 8, 10, 13, 27, 30, 32
    contract/credit ticket, 11–13, 18–19, 23, 27, 30, 79
    organized, 14, 16, 18, 33, 38, 42, 75–76, 111–12
    recruited, xvii, 2, 5, 8, 11, 13–14, 16, 17, 19, 20, 22, 56
    skilled, xviii, 2, 88, 91–92, 98–99, 103–105, 114–15, 124–26, 129, 136, 143–44
World of Suzie Wong, 101
World War I, 23, 45–47, 77
World War II, xviii, 6, 47, 53–54, 58, 64, 73, 78–89, 91, 93–94, 102, 104, 142
Wu, Jason, 133

Y

Yang, C. N., 92
Yasui Minoru, 79, 86
Yasui v. US see court activism
Yellow Peril, xviii, 24, 27–28, 30–31, 39, 78, 81, 118, 133–34, 139–42
Yung Wing, 32, 56

Z

Zhigong Tang, 75